The Devil Made Me Do It Too

The Devil Made Me Do It Too

Pressing, Personal, Poetic Purview

Donald T. Williams

authorHOUSE®

AuthorHouse™
1663 Liberty Drive
Bloomington, IN 47403
www.authorhouse.com
Phone: 1-800-839-8640

First published by AuthorHouse   08/03/2011

ISBN: 978-1-4634-1167-1 (sc)
ISBN: 978-1-4634-1190-9 (hc)
ISBN: 978-1-4634-1189-3 (ebk)

Library of Congress Control Number: 2011908048

Printed in the United States of America

Contents

PSALM 34:18

The lord is close to the brokenhearted. He saves those whose spirits have been crushed.
Unusual, Delusional Trufiction
Fragrant Crucible of Putrid Depression
The Literature of Crisis

Dedication

FYI:

I am what I have been, what I am, and what I ever will be by the Grace of God.

    This book is dedicated to you, the used, abused, and misused "jokes" of the world. You, the so-called "suckers" and "victims" of the self-proclaimed Alpha Dogs and Alpha Wolves of this earth, I bid you now, to regurgitate from the beast's belly as fresh sustenance, the birth of renewed faith. Prey of the ones with the sharpest claws, the deepest reach, food of the ones who never hunger or tire to eat with their ravenous, razor sharp teeth, it is to you I speak. I set aside and immortalize the pages of this literary work in honor of the ducks, lambs, and sheep like me who heretofore were of no notable mention other than that of "maggots" by the self-renowned Alphas. "Maggots" ironically, upon which they, the beast, feed and feast without cease. Sounds confusing to say the . . . This food for thought, I hunger, hope, and pray you'll eat time and time again. Read, regurgitate, and allow your eyes, mind, heart, and soul to nourish and feast again, from beginning to end.

    We, the misused "jokes" of the world, were of no notable mention until a miraculous intervention brought to our attention an opportunity for redemption. This discourse of thought is a mark of respect addressed to the "exploited" of the past, present, and future. Inscribed to those who have been wrongfully used and abused physically, psychologically, and/or emotionally, these voluminous pages of appeal and protest, attest, confess, and profess the pleasures and pains which have been gifted, lifted, shaped, shifted, afflicted, inflicted, conflicted, and liberally restricted by the apathetic hands of fleeting life and time, both cruel and sublime, during the brevity of our enigmatic lives. From these pages, a spirit, beaten yet strengthened, regales odd piety and defiance, "No more compliance and/ or reliance on silence!" The warning "to never speak of such things" is now officially deplored and ignored. The truth will now and forever have the floor as this writer implores the curious, like or unlike minded reader, to explore what my verses have stored in this book's poetic rhythms and chords.

What the so-called "Alphas" have done grieves immensely "the once despicable "persons" or defamed "maggots" like you and me. As our passion comes intensely, it leaves us; we bleed love's hate in our pus as thus. Should you bear, care, or dare to barefoot baby first step mind's eye blind into this tempting snare, its prize most rare, then by all means, please, first strike and proceed; read! Yes, The Spirit Made Me Do It and The Devil Made Me Do It Too. He too, as all of us and everything, from God came. Disobediently evil and ever envious, a Devil he is most certainly, but alas, just a servant answerable to God, Almighty all the same. The Father of Lies can be made, by God, to bare the truth. Do you doubt this? Require proof? Then poof! Watch the Grey Spectre appear and disappear like a space and time inter dimensional spook. This bittersweet pill in book form may make you as sick, scared, and/or hopeful as a cancer patient on chemo. It's up to you to take your medicine, face your demons or die of your disease. Hope you have insurance, a pot to piss in, and a window to throw it out of when it's all said and done. But these luxuries, although a blessing, are by no means a guarantee. Sending up your sincere prayers, on the other hand, increase the probability of a complete recovery or outright miracle, but that's just my bias opinion. Books, liked or disliked, may be a bitter, effective pill or a sweet placebo, but if either treats or heals an evil ill, is that not for the good or better still? If it be God's will, is it not better or best even still? Only God and I actually know what my motifs, motives, and intentions are in this work, but if you read it and its older twin, then I guess your opinion is entitled. The Devil Made Me Do It Too. What forces, good or evil, make you?

Acknowledgments

Acknowledgments usually amount to a list of names and honorable words of gratitude bestowed upon individuals who in some way contributed to the content, craft, or feedback on the final product of a published work. Authors give credit where it is due, anticipated, or expected. Otherwise, people who rendered valuable, support, knowledge, expertise, or assistance, would fail to be duly noted. As with so many other writers, I too am in someone's debt, many someone's actually: family members, friends, associates, colleagues, advisors, and supervisors who by some quirk of fate have been absent of my presence but never unloved or forgotten. Those of you out there, aware or unaware of my love, admiration, respect, and debt, will have to settle for this "cop out" because I'm not sure you'd like to pass on anonymity, be bravely associated with me, step forward, and collect my debt. Not in the case of this "piece of work" or the "piece of work" that wouldn't "cop out" and use a pseudonym.

Don't get me wrong. I'm not ashamed of this literary contribution to society or myself. I'm too subjective and methodical for that. I definitely consider it a "work of art", but because of its tone, language, allegations, and sensitive areas, individuals to whom I owe a debt of gratitude may prefer to remain unnamed, unaccredited, and invisible. The "usual suspects" in what some may consider a criminal offense, will be spared the "perp walk" and "line up" of my identifiable acknowledgments, but nonetheless, share my thanks. This may be for the best. As a quasi, mobile sitting duck, I can prove to be deceptive and elusive to even the most seasoned "grey ghost" guerrilla in the mist. I just don't know my place, tend to speak coherently, and not only ruffle feathers but leave opposing birds of prey without beak, plucked, wings clipped, and talon less. Camouflaged morons hunting them or me receive the same. I don't discriminate. And before my fellow animal lovers cry foul and protest seemingly cruel and unusual punishment, I am obliged to proclaim reprehensively, "I only kill what I eat; they had it coming and have no one to yank but themselves." So, acknowledge that! There shall be no sympathy for the Devil once the Solid Rock begins to rock and roll. How do I know it to be so? A little sparrow with a big Crossbow and plenty arrows told me so. Thanks.

INTRODUCTION

Everybody's heard about and is leery of the wolves in sheep's clothing, but is perhaps a bit complacent and less apprehensive of the latent natural born killers naturally camouflaged in an exterior of innocence that cloaks the guile imbued in all of us, even the most innocent of babes, except One, God's Son. According to the Bible, it's something innately inherent and characteristic in all men and women this thing, I'll call, deceptive sin. Whether you believe in the Bible or not, you must admit that as far as mankind is concerned, sins of all kind are a pervasively prevalent stable of man's daily diet. Some of us nibble at it as if we're conscientiously counting calories and watching our weight. Some of us eat moderately out of value or respect for our probable souls and the remote possibility it may be a commodity of essential value to a deity, if not ourselves. Some of us blatantly gorge ourselves in gluttonous fashion, aspiring to overindulge in the substances of excess and decadence. Perhaps oblivious of any prior religious teaching, warning, or condemnation of seven so-called deadly sins, we copulate as frequently as pigs root at the trough. Bon appétit! Whichever way you bite or slice it, we've all tasted the apple stuffed in the orifice of a table topped swine. That image or that of a naïve naked woman seduced by a persuasive snake in the Garden fails to make the apple any less appealing. Impure to our cores, we continue to consume forbidden fruit, and as a result, ferment in a vinegary state of mental, emotional, and physical turmoil. Present company included, this flesh and bone, walking, talking, condiment is shaping up for the sake of soul preservation. My writing this book may prompt doubt in you about my rigor, vigor, and determination, but it's a long road, I'm just starting out, and have an excellent trainer who is patient, slow to anger, and a blessing to have by my side. That is, if you believe in "such things", and I do.

I know you're not a dimwit as I've heard myself referred to, but I'll identify the "such things" as the following and not rely on inference: the Holy Trinity, the Devil, angels, demons, good, evil, Heaven, Hell, past, present, and future heroes and heretics of the then, now, here, there, hereafter, and afterlife. These are the "whole ball of wax things" of which many of us have belief. We love, hate, revere, fear, count on, and/ or condemn the sight unseen while others deem this "whole ball of wax" the equivalent of a sight seen upper excrement of the body expelled from the ear canal. "How stupid, frightened, gullible, and pathetic can you be?" is the belief between their ears. It supplants the functional secretions of the Biblical glands of God's Word, of which there is no waste. What is a waste is the time devoted to sinful things at our disposal, but don't count this book as sinful time expended carelessly and thoughtlessly. Its appearance as an ill-conceived vendetta for emotional and psychological abuse compounded by significant financial losses may be apparent and true to form. I'll be the first to admit or should I say "confess" that I've gotten even and settled scores before, but I encourage the reader to read beyond a conceivable facade for the tattered remnants of either love lost or lost love and for some vestiges of decency which, as a gentleman, have not completely escaped me. A few of the verses pinned in the poems of this book were written in my preteens and are decades old while others range from a couple of years, a few months, or are brand spanking new. Collectively, they paint a picture, tell a story, and clear the air as I vent. Better raising this hell than raising an even uglier head that's better off (for all) to remain masked. They say, "Good things come to and for those who wait", and I consider this a "good thing", but I'm not some rich, "bleached blonde ambition" in her mansion or production company's kitchen, standing over cauldrons, cooking the books and a full course of white collar crimes for her kind to do a little time and/or get away with scot-free. I don't cook either crack or crystal, but I do tell a whale of a tale and have some even bigger fish to deep fry. By and by and by the way, the dimwit references to me in the past and future have also been modified with the same aforementioned unflattering adjectives. Regardless, I believe in the Holy Trinity lock, stock, and barrel and hence, by faith, affirm the presence and power of God, His counterparts, and as it must be, His contradictors.

Now that it is established that fallible me acknowledges the "whole ball of wax" as the supreme positive thing, I'm about to put my foot in my mouth (no apple for this pig) and "trip up" big time (no acid on my tongue either). However, my confidence, faith, and trust all tell me that my Father will allow it, only to catch me. Fact is, events in this book are a reality for me, but some will quickly dismiss it as tasteless, baseless, and delusional. Written in a moment of simultaneous strength and frailty, this book of poems is one of two un-identical twins whose functions and characteristics bare similarities and differences worthy of a student's analysis in a well thought out and constructed Venn diagram. Look! There goes the retired teacher still giving assignments for a couple of books no public school would offer as part of a curriculum or syllabus, but who knows? I believe God does work in mysterious ways, and I'm full of wishful thinking. This book, what I consider a necessary step forward on my road to redemption, is a very public introspective and retrospective confession of past and/or current sins I've committed or at least thought about committing. It is an airing of my dirty laundry and clean clearing of the skeletons in my closet; a twofold confessional-like testimonial and a "civil" response to my "real" or "perceived as real" family betrayal, conspiracy, and crimes against me by a cohort of strangers who were revealed to me by their arrogance. Take it or leave it at or for its worth. Let it plant a seed in your mind, fertile ground of immeasurable girth.

Many will say, "He's crazy!" and many more may consider the contents of this book the blasphemous, "tacky" work of the Devil as its title suggests, but if it sticks to you or you stick to it, it's all relative and relevant. Where the bones and dust settle is of importance to me because I must be thorough before I close the door or endeavor to ever open it again. Right now, I can barely trust anyone other than God himself, and I believe that's the way He wants it. The conflicting thought that no man is an island makes this lone wolf think of compromise and some highly desired female companionship, but I have trust issues made apparent by one or two poems within this book. Read for yourself. I'm having one hell of a pity party. Can't you hear the melancholy whine of a melodious violin's strings sing, "Poor, poor Donald; poor sitting duck ran out of luck; became the hapless victim of "those people" who don't give a fuck!"? I wrote it but don't like this music or the rap songs and other tunes sung about me by various artists during 2006 and 2007. Yeah, I know what you're thinking, "He "is" delusional". My doctors certainly think so. What a complete misconception or possible misdiagnosis! Unbeknown to me, I could be living, yet another lie. Once a sinner, always a sinner and once a liar, always a liar is what I've always been told. We all could be living a lie in life's prerecorded reality play. This untrained "could have been, should have been" actor and legend in his own mind has always thought he had the world fooled or believed it should have been according to my script. Everyone, except my dear, departed mother. "You're a thief, a liar, and you're going to die on the gallows!" was what she would often admonishingly confide in me after I was busted for this, that, or the other, and I never cared for that unhappy ending. Honestly, I was awed and annoyed by her keen listening skills, powers of observation, and accuracy in keeping track of her money down to the penny, but it never deterred me. The tears of an anguished mother and father only meant that I'd stop stealing from them. Besides, they were on to me, and by age twelve, I needed more cash than I could "night crawl withdrawal" from her purse and his pockets to bank roll my park gambling and love for eating lunch in diners daily. Not until after I read a stolen Bible four years ago and made an attempt to come clean with God, myself, and others, did I decide to play it straight for once and turn over a new leaf. Not that anyone was ever fooled by antics anyhow; I never really tried to hide anything except for my pain. Publishing this book after The Spirit Made Me Do It is a contradiction and little indication of any leaf turning, but it, like me, has a positive purpose. The social commentary laced here and there are things I felt compelled to voice, and like it or not, I'll flex my "right to free speech" muscles as much as I like and as much as any other "bigots" I know, since I've had my Privacy, Civil Rights, and Constitutional Rights violated by "those people", Law Enforcement, and the Judicial System. Those who did it, were compliant, or condoned it, know I speak the truth. You also know I'm a well-educated gentleman, but just beneath the venerable veneer is the same crystal clear, yet opaque rogue who has always fancied himself a double agent, working both sides of these mean streets long before he ever saw an espionage film, carried heat, picked up a Bible, found Jesus, or Jesus found him. This book is a product of Grey Spectre Enterprises LLC, of which I have personally sworn, is "In His Majesty's Service", and it's no secret.

Neither secret is the belief that God works in mysterious ways beyond our simple understanding nor is the fact that the "smartest guys in the room" have a pompously ignorant inability to accept their low position on the totem pole of God's grand scheme and scale of life, reality, time, space, and the Universe. Atheists and agnostics want to be in the game, coach, ride the bench, cheer, be in the stands, watch from home or the sports bar, and Tivo at the same time. Impossible, but they'll believe that before they'll acknowledge God. You better get with the right program and with the winning team, smarty pants. Cruel and repugnantly vile things happen to good and bad people alike, and we ask ourselves how or why God would allow it? Natural disasters and those caused by man himself occur and we ask the same question or blame it on the work of the Devil. So, Lucifer's out and about doing his thing, and there's "not" a God Almighty out there too, first and foremost, calling all the shots, yinging some Chinaman's yang (Yeah, He's got time for that, even the little things.), and getting angrier by the nanosecond because you hard heads can't see the light? Satan makes the perfect "fall guy" in ways that aren't mysterious but obvious. "Evil", you'll acknowledge, but you doubt the Father, the Son, and the Holy Spirit when there's far more "Goodness" all about you. Even when his handiwork is subtle or less apparent, the role of scapegoat fits Lucifer suitably. Almighty God, who has a far greater repertoire, bag of goodies, up his sleeve miracles, arsenals, blessings, or disasters should be acknowledged by everyone and everything, living or dead as exactly that, God Almighty. Start of story. End of tale. As with my first book, I again, felt myself compelled and driven by a power greater than me, a power ultimately for good. So again, don't let the title of this one completely fool or mislead. I believe it's all about temptation with the Devil, and he can't "make" you do anything. It's been proven to me that nothing in life's fair. All I offer in "fair play" is conformity to the established rules of English. I may flash a badge of poetic license to kill in my attempt to bring to literary justice "those people" who wronged me, violated the rite and rights of marriage, and as well, my aforementioned rights: Privacy, Civil, and Constitutional. If anything goes when you go rogue, it's my right to hit high or below the belt. My head and center mass loose cannon bipolar rants serve as a verbal blunder bust just short of the real thing. Every once and a while, I'll shoot a blank "Cloze" to the target, but that's just to keep the reader engaged and demonstrate leniency. (It's an old school Reading teacher thing, very old school) Granted, "those people" in my sights, will never see the inside of a jail or a courtroom from a captured criminal's perspective anyway because if they're not the law, they are rich enough to be above it so I've been sanctioned to put them down. To them, I was no more than a passing joke, someone to be taken advantage of, someone to go home and laugh at and about, but I am so much more than that according to my Father, the only One I trust and believe. And even with this book, I hope to please. How ironic! And, oh yeah, I know you thought "moronic".

The "feint" of free choice and free will, must make us a humorously interesting pastime for God Almighty. We, sinners at birth unaware of the ruse, are manipulated like chess pieces on a sacred chessboard. All moves, all actions anticipated, foreseen, and preordained by Him in the End Game of His creation and design, played out on a trillion boards of heavenly bodies. Consider this another strategy, another mysterious way by the Highest Power to get your attention in case the first twin slipped by you unnoticed. As good and as evil as this world is, the probability of this book serving His purpose is more than favorable considering that God moves in mysterious ways; even though it may appear that The Devil Made Me Do It Too. And/or I'm just plain crazy.

PART ONE
ESSENCE AND EXTRACT

THIS IS

By Donald T. Williams

This is my story
And what went wrong
I take the blame
With me, it belongs

This is my story
And what went wrong
Beg for forgiveness
And strength to move on

I can do well
I can do poorly
Somehow therein,
Both times I've had surely

Savings
And
Squander
I have known

Eagles
Have landed
Nest eggs
Have flown

I once knew love
I now know alone
From my goodness and sins
I've learned and grown

That's not to say
Doing wrong is good,
But one learns from mistakes
As it is

The hard lessons teach well
As they should

What lies beyond the earthen, clay vessel?
God only knows
Stands me transformed by the potter
For all to behold

Donald T. Williams

USEFUL USE

By Donald T. Williams

You may feel betrayed?
You may be dismayed?
How can a man who prays
Use profanity this way?

You may feel disgust
Ask,
"Who can you trust?"
Know that it's only God
Owner of mercy and of the rod

As Grey Spectre,
I do as I'm told
Holy Spirit told me so;
It's a "GO!"
Don't hold back your tongue
HGS songs must be sung

Sung in a way
Both sides understand
I am for God Almighty,
Holy Spirit most grand

Jesus, God's Son,
Is our Shepherd
We, mere mortal men,
Are His sheep
God
Has given His Word
God
Vows to keep

White sheep or black
And all in between

Will come to know
Understand
What God means

What cuts mustard
What God despises
Listen to these poems
As Grey Spectre desires,

Without compromise,
To convey to you
All of what God has said
Is true
Repent now
Before you are through

You may feel angry
You may agree
Or
Disagree
That I have professed God,
And, or, but
That I have professed falsely

Grey Spectre's
Just a tool
In an infinite box
Grey Spectre's
A cute rabbit
Grey Spectre's
A sly fox

Grey Spectre's
A bitten tongue
Poked in a busted cheek
Grey Spectre's
A raging river
Grey Spectre's
A dried up creek

Vague,
Oxymoronic rogue,
Cloudy,
Mystery man of defaced deceit,
Supernatural,
Subliminal wannabe,
Misguided, misty vapors
Of pompous conceit

Similes and metaphors
Make a fine figurative fix
Like a slow boat to China
Masquerades
As a ride down the River Stix

Sure as night
Gives way to day
Grey Spectre may trick
Or play charades

Please stick with the text
That is most agreeable to you
Grey Spectre reaches out to all
Doing as told to do

I'm merely a mortal man;
Grey Spectre's a portal, man
Playthings
Of and for God
We
Seek His approval,
An affirmative nod

Methods diverse,
Means to an end
Implicit
And
Explicit
As a porn diva's behind,
I do as I'm told

Making useful use
Of biding my time

You may feel betrayed?
You may be dismayed?
How can a man who prays
Use profanity this way?

You may feel disgust,
Ask
"Who can you trust?"
Know that it's only God,
Owner of mercy and of the rod

Voiceless pantomime's screams beseech,
"Holy Father you must reach!"
Deafened ears crammed to the max
With the Devil's lies and crap
Trapped between the temples
That God holds dear
Excavate
That they may hear

By any means necessary
Means you care
Grey Spectre's voice
Is clear,
A breath
Of funky fresh,
Unfiltered
Air

You may feel betrayed?
You may be dismayed?
How can a man who prays
Use profanity this way?

You may feel disgust?
Ask,
"Who can you trust?"

Know that it's only God,
Owner of mercy and of the rod

Grey Spectre
And
I
Do as told
Holy Spirit sanctioned
So,
It's a "Go!"
Take them up,
Down,
Through,
And
Around!
Don't hold back your tongue
HGS songs
Must be sung

Sung in a way
Both sides understand
I am for God Almighty,
Holy Spirit,
Most Grand

I DESPISE

By Donald T. Williams

I despise
The Father of Lies
Who constantly
Tries to get inside

To get inside
My mind and heart
To convince me
From God depart

Doubt the Father
And myself
Risk my spirit
Risk my health

Risk my soul
For all eternity
If the serpent
Plants the seed

I despise
The wicked ways
I pity
Those who disobey

I was one
Of them before
Now I try
To sin no more

Imperfect man
As could ever be,
Yet,

Sin has no zest,
Appeal for me

Transformation
In correct effect
Trinity
I give thrice respect

Cast aside
The wicked ways
Give my God
Relentless praise

In God's Armor
I am cloaked
Speak to me
The Devil chokes

I despise
The Father of Lies
I despise
The tricks he tries

I despise
The serpent's tongue
Songs that hiss
Should not be sung

Yet, I may be
Guilty of this
Not as holy
As I wish

Holy Spirit
Told me so?
Did the Devil
Have a role?

Grey Spectre says,
"Please ponder this.
Arrows may hit

Arrows may miss
Lips may lie
Lips may kiss
Double duty
For this
Double duty
For that
Double duty
For tit
Double duty
For tat

White and black
Mix up as grey
Dual edge sword
In words I say

Lies
Therein
The truest truth
As with God
Therein
Lies
Proof"

Get the point?
Did Jesus bleed?
Will you now give in?
Will you now concede?

That all I say
Has relevance to you
That God is great,
That Jesus is due?

I despise
The wicked ways
Pity those
Those who disobey

Imperfect man
As could ever be
Yet,
Sin has no zest,
Appeal for me

Transformation
In correct effect
Trinity
I give thrice respect

Cast aside
The wicked ways
Give my God
Relentless praise

TRUFICTION

By Donald T. Williams

Is this truth?
Is this fiction?
Witless babble
Born of addiction?

Born of physical illness
And mental disease,
Born of abuse
Or of attention's need?

Call it
Vengeance,
A need to kick ass
Call it
Anal retention
Or constipation that won't pass

Call it
A colonoscopy
Call it
Beano proof gas
Call it
An enema
For an _____ ass

Sweet truth
As I know it
Or
Imaginative,
Creative,
Pretense
Impaired of mind?

Either way,
I,
As the wind,
Ring chimes

Either way,
I,
As the hurricane's eye,
See beyond seas
To ghostly write of crimes

Crimes
Against nature
Crimes
Against man
Mystery meat
Examined
Once dropped out of the can

How can you
Compete with this?
Take the truth
To twist your wrists

Into complete submission
You must fall
Such is the case
When Grey Spectre calls

Calls you
On your evil ways
Calls to say
Crime doesn't pay

Misty, Grey Spectre
Rides the breeze
Makes you crumble,
Humbly to your knees

Is this truth?
Is this fiction?

Witless babble
Born of addiction?

Born of physical illness
And mental disease,
Born of abuse
Or of attention's need?

Sweet truth
As I know it
Or
Imaginative,
Creative,
Pretense
Impaired of mind?

Either way,
I,
As the wind,
Ring chimes

Either way,
I,
As the hurricane's eye,
See beyond the seas
To ghostly write of crimes

Crimes
Against nature
Crimes
Against man
Mystery meat
Examined
Once dropped out of the can

"Trufiction"
Could be the word
Explanation
Of what your mind has heard

Take as truth
Or
As grain of salt
Either way
These crimes shall halt

Sooner
Or
Later
A price to be paid
Mark my words
And count your days

How can you
Compete with this?
Take the truth
To twist your wrists

Make you squirm
I must insist
How you've gone
And gotten me pissed!

Grey Spectre's mind
Permeates the breeze
Goes where there's want
Goes where there's need

How can you
Compete with this?
Tame the wind
Or tame the mist?

Either way
I,
As the wind,
Ring chimes

Either way
Grey Spectre
And
I
Expose crimes

How can you
Compete with this mind twister?
Dropped your cards
At Absolute Blister

THIS IS WHO I AM

By Donald T. Williams

I'm the living,
Urban legend
Unknown poet
Who keeps them guessing

Only the "In Crowd" underground
Have ever heard of me
They know my lyrics
And personal history

Nosey,
Stealing motherfuckers
Down low freaks,
Male cocksuckers

Rappers, hustlers, pimps
And
Wangsters with a "G"
All up in my business
Cause: Their envy

But,
I'll have the final word,
Spitfire the final song,
Have some fat bitch
Sing along in a thong
But,
It won't be my swan song

This is who I am
Donald T. Williams
Chilly D. Williams
Aka Donnie C, Son of Tom and Ann

An extraordinary guy
Trying to live an ordinary life
Earth bound star
With a luminous, inner light

This is who I am
Man child of the Promised Land
Always doing more than enough
But not as much as he can

Son of a King
Noble of birth
Heir to seeds and spoils
Of his God's Earth

Most men nightmares
Most women's dream
Quiet noise
And silent scream

Yes,
I'm one sick puppy
To say the least
Can't control me
I'm best unleashed

Heard them call me D Boy,
Street Runner, and the like
Hauling ass on 95
Gunning up and down the East Coast Turnpike

What's this 'bout me hauling drugs?
Niggers know I don't do that
Ain't nobody's fool or mule,
And that's a fact

Yes,
I've blown some bucks
How many bottles of beer or booze
Have you sucked?

Donald T. Williams

Suck on a bottle,
Pull on a cigar, cigarette, or a joint
All are addictions
So, what's your point?

Scorch a pipe
Or powder your nose
Take a trip
Let your mind go

Yes,
I've flicked my fair share of Bics
There's much truth in that,
But "we" can all get clean;
Ask Him;
God can help you with that

I E D

By Donald T. Williams

I never rehearse
What I say
When it comes,
It comes that way

Like a horse
With an unbridled mouth
I run Mustang free
Without a mount

Strong
As ever and footloose
Tongue's a muzzle
If I choose

So don't try
To muzzle me
Cut you down
If cutting is what you need

I'm an I E D
On
Each side and middle of the road
Crossing me
Can take a really serious toll

I'm an I E D
Remotely controlled
I'm an I E D
Ready and primed to explode

Tripwire
Poised before your path

Tread on me
And that's your ass

Triquetrous, double-edged claymores
Box you in on three sides
Better back out tail between,
Better run and hide

Pull the trigger
Pull the wire
Find yourself
Under heavy fire

Verbal barrage
Like a Pistol Pete
Best to run
Best to retreat

Think about what you have done
Beg to see another sun
Otherwise, accept your fate
Equal measure, hate for hate

Improvised explosive device
Donnie C's nasty and cold as ice
Bringing the heat underneath your feet
Bringing you death beneath your seat

Raise the white flag,
And I'll end this war,
Or I'll continue to slay
And never get bored

Grey Spectre's a ghost
With an awesome will
Grey Spectre's a spirit
That you can't kill

Donnie C's a persona
Five decades old

Telling a story
In truth and bold

If you have a problem
With what I say,
Shout "Oh, nigger, please behave!"
If you wish for me the grave

There's no way
I plan or plant to do that
On my words,
I do stand pat

I never rehearse
What I say
When it comes,
It comes that way

I'm an I E D
Remotely controlled
I'm an I E D
Ready and primed to explode
I
Am
An
Inspirational
Educational
Device
Designed for you
To disarm and decode

Learn Life and English Lessons
Live by Grey Spectre's Motto:

___ __ __ _____

___ __ __ ___ __ ___

DONNIE C's SHOES

By Donald T. Williams

I'm the nigga
Donnie C picked
To fill his shoes

Inside niggas know
Donnie C don't rap
He's more into rhythm and blues

Play some old school doo wop
Donnie C's
Good to go

Play some White boys hard rock
Donnie C
Will explode

Play some Jimi Hendrix for him
Donnie C's
A big fan

As far as Donnie C's concerned
Jimi Hendrix was and still is
The Man

Guitar riffs from him
And major White boy hits
Always had his ear

Roaring down some open highway
Or old country road
Donnie C's cranking, shifting mad "air" gears

Nothing he likes more
Than fast cars
And dope sound

Donnie C's
Got a baker's dozen tickets
For the way he throws down

Donnie C's
Like James Caan
In that movie Thief

Ill legit hustler
Changing cars like shoes
For every day of the week

I'm the nigga
Donnie C picked
To spitfire his songs

I'm the nigga
Donnie C picked
To deal with the crowds and the throngs

Donnie C's so hot
So many irons in the fire
Nigga had to farm out work to the best guns for hire

Gave you all the low
Inside edition scoop
You're gonna get

Just cause Donnie C called on me,
And I responded with respect and correct
Doesn't mean I'm the teacher's pet

Believe me home boys
And home girls
That ain't such a bad thing

Being teachers' pets
Just means
You really want graduation rings

School bell has rung
School is so cool
Button up, listen, respect one another, and obey the rules

Donnie C's words
Can be rapped
You might want to sing

Recite
As The Spoken Word
As when poets do their thing

Donnie C's
The urban legend
That most folks don't know

Hear me rap about him,
Legend in his own mine for all time,
Doesn't want to star bright, spotlight in his show

Nigga's got me as if a font, fronting and flowing
Like a fountain pen, man
Spitting rhymes in a way Donnie My Boy's urban legend keeps
growing

Will Smith,
I am Legend,
I'm sure you all know

Donnie C's a big fan
And Will Smith
He don't personally know

One of Donnie C's best friends,
Roosevelt,
Lives in Philly

So, it's like some sick,
Six degrees of Kevin Krisp Bacon shit
If Donnie C says so

As sure as
The sun also rises
And genuine stars fill the sky

Donnie C's
Light will shine
In the sweet by and by

Donnie C,
The so called "Pprophett 4 Pprofitt
Can but won't drop it or stop it"

Donnie C,
"The PProphett 4 PProfitt"
Will be an urban legend in everyone's eyes

DONNIE MY BOY

By Donald T. Williams

Donnie My Boy
Can write some shit
Each one penned
Is a bona fide hit

Donnie My Boy
Now, he don't spit
But most rappers
Love his shit

John Wayne's Rooster Cockburn
Has True Grit
The straight shooting Shootist
Drew fast and hit

Cut from the same tough cloth
Off the block came the chip
Donnie My Boy got more hits
Than you suckers can lick

Took a long time for Donnie C
To come around
Took a long time for Donnie C
To come down

Always knew there wasn't ass
That he could not kick
Always knew there ain't a drug
That he can't lick

Donnie C lost a lot of time
Hurting inside
Always had a anger
That was real hard to hide

Self medication let him
Numb it that way,
But a life on drugs
Is going to cause some decay

Yet, Donnie My Boy
Could always write some shit
Put a pen to paper
And he don't know how to quit

Time to rock the world
With some creative wit hits
Some are nice and decent
Some came straight out of the pit,

But Donnie My Boy
Can write some shit
Donnie My Boy
Is going to cause some fits

That's Donnie My Boy
Man of style,
Man of wit

Love him?
Hate him?
Take your pick

SELF FULFILLING PROPHECY

By Donald T. Williams

As a young boy,
My mother would often tell me
Something about myself
I somehow already knew
She told me it so often
Her words
I came to believe were true

As a young boy,
My father also had something to say
Heard it from him so often,
I can hear his voice today

Did they say
These things out of meanness,
Were my own parents
Being cruel?

It told me something
About this world
If you hear something long enough,
What you hear,
For you,
May become truth

Self fulfilling prophecy
Is
What the educators say
Fill a child's mind with bullshit
And
That bullshit is here to stay

"You're a thief and a liar
And

On the gallows is how you'll go"
Heard my mommy say it
So,
They're words I've come to know

Once the seed was planted
It grew from me like a black rose
Power of Suggestion
Or
The devilish path I chose?

My father called me stupid,
But
I knew I wasn't a complete dumbass
Or
Lame
Love and tough love
In my house
Built a sound foundation
For my frame

Always
Had a mean streak
If you hit me,
I'm going to hit you back
Never
Been a punk ass
When it comes to courage,
I don't lack

Made myself a promise
And
That's by the gallows
I won't go
Caught between the crosshairs
Is probably the way
But
Only my God knows for sure

As a young boy,
My mother would often tell me

Something about myself
I somehow already knew
She told me it so often
Her words
I came to believe were true

As a young boy,
My father also had something to say
Heard it from him so often,
I can hear his voice today

Did they say
These things out of meanness,
Were my own parents
Being cruel?

It told me something
About this world
If you hear something long enough,
What you hear,
For you,
May become truth

Self fulfilling prophecy
Is
What educators say
Fill a child's mind with bullshit
And
That bullshit is here to stay

Listen up
Dear children
When cruel words
Are said to you

Listen up
To your higher mind,
Tune out the venomous noise
That poison
Has an antidote
Prayers help you avoid

God
Is talking to you
Hear only
The whispers of your heart
Telling you
You're priceless,
Starlight in the dark

Telling you
You're someone
Worthy of His love
That you have within you
The power to rise above

Star high
Above the harsh words
Designed to pull you down
Words designed to rob you
To steal away your crown

ST. JOHN'S

By Donald T. Williams

Pulled on my legs
Pressed your foot on my groin
Laughed as you pulled harder
Snapped the veins in my loins

St. John's Park
Was the place of sports
Big Fat John
Was the black overcoat cloaked pork

Teenage gangster in a black Fedora
Was an unusual sight
Friend, who publically, physically abused me
Revealed the twisted, sadistic cruelty of life

Bullies in the park
Have been my prey since those days
Sure, I came to ball,
But there were other games I'd play

Getting even
Stopped my inner grieving
Face to face
Or face to back

Dispensing greater pain
Can be relieving
And there's no stopping
My counterattack

It may come today
It may come tomorrow
Setting fire to my ire
Brings you nothing but sorrow

Hard lessons learned early
Prepare you for what's to come
Friends may appear aplenty
Perhaps "they" are not "one" among

The lone wolf keeps no company
Suppose that's for the best
Packs are packed full of envy
Vying for domination over the rest

The lone wolf's preservation
Relies on courageous inner strength, wits, and guile
Virtues most advantageous
When contending with the vile

St. John's Park is a testing ground
Always has been a special place
Countless neighboring youth have risen or fallen there
As they handballed, softballed, three pointed, or raced

Years and generations
Offer up as valid proof
Kids learn life lessons at home, church, school,
Or under a community's Rec. Center's roof

St. John's Park and Recreation Center
Were alive and well back in the day
Hope and pray, I dare say
Both live still, yet not the same way

Pulled on my legs
Pressed your foot on my groin
Laughed as you pulled harder
Snapped the veins in my loins

St. John's Park
Was the place of sports
Big Fat John
Was the black overcoat cloaked pork

Teenage gangster in a black Fedora
Was an unusual sight

Donald T. Williams

Friend, who publically, physically abused me,
Revealed the twisted, sadistic cruelty of life

Big Fat Johns
Still root and stalk the parks and streets,
But the weakest prey is stronger
When he's packing an Equalizer's heat

Yes! No!
This should
Or should not be
But alas, it is reality

Zip guns
Now, replaced with AKs and Nines
Same old ghetto
Different, yet similar times

Bullies come in every gender and race
Adults must reach, teach, preach and/or put them in their proper
place
Protect the mild child; keep him/her safe
Cease the real and cyber threats, beats, suicides, and murder rates

Getting even
Stops the grieving?
Face to face
Face to back?

There's no stopping counterattack?
A life taken can't come back?
Understanding and compassion are what we lack?
If I turn my cheek, will the other get smacked?

Big Fat Johns
Still root and stalk the parks and streets
But the littlest child is wrong and strong
When he's/she's backing the biggest heat

Surely,
There is another way

Two way mirrors
Reveal truth
But
Falsely convey

Hindsight's reflection
Is not always Windex clear
Images in the rear view
Are closer than appear

Today's man in the mirror
Can't look the other way
Today's man in the mirror
Is man enough to say

We'd be wise
To kneel
We'd be prudent
To pray

Surely,
The Father,
The Son,
The Holy Spirit

And
St. John

Will bless us
And
Our children's days

Will show us love,
Love
Is God's right way

SCORPIO

By Donald T. Williams

Donnie C
Is a Scorpio
Most people know
What that means
Donnie C's
An insect
Donnie C's
A King

Lucky
If you know one
Unlucky
If you cross
Don't want
To see his dark side
Don't want
To have to pay that cost

Donnie C
Minds his business
Keeps
Pretty much to himself
Don't get in his business
With his business
Better not mess

Some fools
Don't heed warning
For their own good,
They don't care

Messing around
In Donnie C's business
Is like fucking
With a Grizzly Bear

Donnie My Boy
Will maul
You
Separate
You
Limb
By
Limb
Donnie My Boy
Will destroy
You
Don't matter
How much you hit the gym

Eat
Your ass for breakfast
Pass
Your ass as gas by noon
Shit
You the next morning
Look
For someone else to consume

Donnie C's
A Scorpion
Even the dumbest nigger
Should know
No matter which way
Donnie C's going
That's not the way
You want to go

Donnie C's
A Scorpion
His stinger's cocked and primed
To go

Best you
Walk wide around him
His touch
You don't want to know

Unless,
You're a fine lady
Of good heart,
Brains
And
Intentions too

Best you too
Walk wide around Donnie C
He'll have little
Or
Nothing
To do with you

Donnie C
Is a Scorpio
Most people know
What that means
Donnie C's
An insect
Donnie C's
A King

Lucky
If you know him
Unlucky
If you cross

Don't want
To see his dark side
Don't want
To pay that cost

TRIPPING

By Donald T. Williams

He came to me
On an acid trip
As a teenage boy,
I wanted to be hip

Jimi Hendrix and the Rolling Stones
Pounding in my brain
Drugs were "my thing"
Making the "ordinary" change

Daily excursions
Became my norm
Convinced that I could handle
Didn't see the harm

Hid it from my parents
Kept up grades and kept a job
Didn't really dawn on me
How many brain cells I would rob

Bugging out on a Project's bench
Passing past my curfew time
Caught up in a twilight
With no stars in sky to find

Cloudy skies soon parted
And I said, "How can this be?"
Saw a ghostly skull face
Staring down at me

That's the very evening
The Grey Spectre made himself known
Said that he'd be with me
Never leave me alone

"Go about your business,
But I'll come for you one day.
Give you revelations
About the life you have portrayed."

Rip Van Winkle sleepwalking
Then one day, I awoke
Bubble I had slept in
Burst when the "snow" globe broke

Living lies comes easy
When you find the truth too hard
Unlocked doors are easily opened
When you leave the door ajar

The Devil needs no invitation
Like his bloodthirsty vampires do
All he needs is a flaw, crimp, dent, crack,
Or the very holes in you

Pores may be the smallest
Orifices liken wide open gates
Why and how well you protect them
Will tell of your eternal fate

Cloudy skies now parted
I now know how this can be
Story written so long ago,
And I how I love the mysteries!

"Go about your business,
But I'll come for you one day.
Give you revelations
About the life you have portrayed."

Nothing like a Sherlock
With a lock too hard to pick
The impossible is possible
As a Mad Hatter and his tricks

Rabbit holes lie open
Underworlds are easily probed

Best you guard your secrets
Buckle belts and tighten robes

"Go about your business,
But I'll come for you one day.
Give you revelations
About the life you have portrayed."

Multi trips on acid,
Peyote, mescaline, and such,
Defects in a man-child character
Who doesn't give a fuck?

Reefers, coke, and crack
Fine citizens never make
Better off with cops as robbers
CO's, lawyers, and Judges on the take

"Carte blanche" Wall Street bankers
With fat, pig pockets too deep to fail
U.S. Treasury printing more trillions
For the next inevitable, "shrewd" bankers' bail

White collar crimes
Never dirty
The linen closet Klansmen's
Pristine sheets

Bleach
Makes his gin and tonic
Makes pot farming, pharming,
And
Pharmaceutics money laundering
A grand scale feat

Makes for wishes of a colorless country
How's that for a "pipe dream" most cruel?
Pit countrymen against each other
As brothers in a senseless duel

When all the while,
Predators and Reapers at remote controlled ready

Nuclear Silos
Impossible to breach

If an untested quarterback President
Makes the wrong call,
Fumbles the "Football",
You'd better hold onto your box or bleacher seats

How does one
Kill an enemy?
Kill an enemy
One can't reach?

As "all" races
Run in canter
Against on ageless
Salamander

Never small
Never weak
Flies the Dragon to the finish line
Of deceit

How does one
Kill an enemy?
Kill an enemy
One can't reach?

Take the "Book"
In a nook
Read of it
I beseech

The Devil needs no invitation
Like his bloodthirsty vampires do
All he needs is a flaw, crimp, dent, crack,
Or the very holes in you

"Go about your business,
But I'll come for you one day.
Give you revelations
About the life you have portrayed."

Came he to me, again
To this now sober mind of mine
Just as real as seconds
Are an abstract unit of time

Eerie words imagined or spoken
Remain with me today
Took some time to grow up,
But every dog must have its day

There are different versions
Of how one comes to grip
Some guys take the long way home
And enjoy the scenic trip

DONNIE CRYSTAL

By Donald T. Williams

Donnie Crystal
Clean as a pistol
Whew! Whew! Whew! Whew! Whew!

When the girls pass,
He's gonna whistle
Whew! Whew! Whew! Whew! Whew!

See that "Rump Roast" passing by
You can bet he'll grab his fly
And whew!
Whew! Whew! Whew! Whew! Whew!
Whew! Whew! Whew! Whew!

Wasting no time with his line
Whew! Whew!
Whew! Whew! Whew! Whew!

Tells that girl she's "super" fine
Whew! Whew!
Whew! Whew! Whew! Whew!

Like an angler with his hooks
Snags a great catch with his looks
No, ain't no one who got away
If a prize stops, she's gonna stay

Whew! Whew,
Whew! Whew! Whew! Whew! Whew!
Whew! Whew! Whew! Whew!

Going with him to his home
Whew! Whew!
Whew! Whew! Whew! Whew!

Girl can see he's on the bone
Whew! Whew!
Whew! Whew! Whew! Whew!

Now that they're alone in bed
It's time to go head to head
Whew! Whew!
Whew! Whew! Whew! Whew! Whew!

But Donnie
Acts real funny
After
The loving
Has been made

He used her
And confused her
Like an old car
He's ready
To trade her away

So if you're out
And hear a whistle,
Whew!
Whew! Whew! Whew! Whew!

You can bet
That's Donnie Crystal
Whew!
Whew! Whew! Whew! Whew!

With that pistol
In his pants
You poor girls
Don't stand a chance

Against Donnie
Donnie Crystal
Out there with that whistle
And his pistol

Talkin' 'bout Donnie Crystal
What a pistol!
Blowin' home girls down
With a whistle

Clear as crystal
Talkin' 'bout Donnie Crystal
See right through him,
Sighted or blind
Ripe, funky, fresh fruit
Straight from the vine
Fine as wine,
All the time

HARD AS A ROCK

By Donald T. Williams

I'm hard as a rock
Why don't you feel my cock?

Of course, that won't do
How about I stick it in you?

Now, don't be afraid
No need for alarm

I was built for love
And I mean you no harm

Won't be no shame
If you scream out my name

Call me Donnie C.
A wet woman's dream

So go on and scream
As I draw you near

Back you up to me
And throw my thing in gear

I was built for speed
From low to high gear

Go on and scream!
That's what I like to hear

I'm as hard as a rock
Why don't you suck my cock?

Use that head of yours
My key opens all doors

Those in front and in back
There ain't a safe I can't crack

I was built for speed
I'm a high speed drill

I mean you no harm
And I'll do you no ill

I'm here to love
I'm here to thrill

Lay down with me
Let me warm up your chill

I'm hard as a rock
Why don't you feel my cock?

Of course, that won't do
How about I stick it in you?

I, ALONE

By Donald T. Williams

He's dead
I don't know his name
She's dead

I,
Alone,
As father,
Am to blame

"You sexless bastard"
Words
Cursed from her bittersweet lips
Young and full of vigor,
But my rocket failed to lift

Lift
Her belly button
Inflate
With watery life
How could one so tender
Wield a tongue as knife?

Claim to love me
As girlfriend,
As fiancée,
As ___

Neither
Was the virgin
Each
Knew full well what to expect
Nor
Were we without equal urging
Our love would merge

But
"Essentially"
Not connect

Spontaneous combustion
Liquid fire
Time and again
My loins were inspired,
But my love and_____ were marred with sin

Load and reload
Failed to explode
Oh, how I pulled the trigger,
But the gunslinger's bravado
Soon
Began to erode

Alas,

Conception finally came,
But my sweet, "Tender Roni" had changed
Had to leave home first,
Live in "her" apartment,
Lift her skirt

Conception finally came!
As did
Morning sickness,
Doubt's dagger,
And love's inevitable pain
Equivalent to the loss is the gain
We're back together again!

But
Both are tainted
Permanent
The stain

How dubious,
How splendid
The first!

I love her so
As the seed does love the earth,
But
Am I true father of our long awaited birth?
Wanting
Someone,
Something
So badly
Can lead to something
Better or worse

Especially,
If you "hear" something that pains you so,
You bury the hurt in a subconscious coffin
Like an evil spell or a curse

Evil
Lives
In many places
In the mind, heart, and mouth

No space
Is more devastating
Than the split tongue
Of a "good intentions" _____

Evil
Lives
Among us
In places we think safe
Just because you think it
A "Happy, Home Sweet Home"
Doesn't mean it's not debased

The one thousandth day
Of love and sex
Life anew
Did begin
Baby's first breath,
A fragrant bouquet,

A lift
From Heaven's wind

Seers know
What's around the bend
Read the river's current
Before events begin

Took a chance,
Knew I should not,
Read the palm
With its lifeline plot

If a man's life
Is written in his hand,
I'm going to live my way,
Rewrite my story
Or at least,
See if I can

Story shared
I,
Alone,
Dared to ignore
Questioned the validity
Of what was "said" to be in store

A baby's breath seed,
Riding the tip of thunder's saber,
Sliced through life's clouds, rains, and fickle winds
Lightning dug the seed deep
Struck twice
Did life's spark
Again

Conception came calling
The one thousand fiftieth day
Of love and sex,
But,
Life
Did

End
Before baby's first breath

Snatched
Sucked
Severed
Before baby's life could progress
Strayed
Swayed
Stayed
The first seven years
Sustained
The "Questionable"
Yet,
Immaculate first

One
Drop of life
Had "quenched"
Drought's thirst

The one thousand fiftieth day
Of love and sex
At last,
Conception came calling

Alas,

I,
Alone,
As father,

Snuffed
The precious life
Of the next

Dear, sweet babe
In Heaven
Waits
For you and me
Waits

To hug his Mommy
Waits
To sit on her Daddy's knee
Oh,
So young and foolish

I,
Alone,
Squandered
Life's most precious gift

Prayers
Had been answered
Granted
Was a sacred wish

Cloudy conscience
Could not see,
Failed to feel,
Sweet babe's breath,
Life, love, pain, and misery

Overly self-concerned
About "buying a home",
Cars,
Material things,
And family finances,

I,
Alone,
As father,
Slew
Sweet babe's
Life and chances

Had life's mega jackpot numbers,
Fell asleep on the job
So deep
The slumber,
The thief in the night,

By himself,
Was robbed

Failed to act
When it counted most
Grey Spectre
Speaks
Of
A sweet babe
Ghost
Who loves me
Nonetheless
The most
Of most

Alas,

I,
Alone,
As father,
Should have,
Could have,
Handled
All
This

Plus
An
Additional,
Unintentional,
Unconditional,
Less
"Dubious"
Bliss

Oh,
So young and foolish

I,
Alone,
As father

Squandered
Life's most precious gift

Now,
That I am older and wiser
I make for us
One
Wish

That in the Great Hereafter
Aborted
Lives, souls, and spirits
Exist
Forever
In God's grace

Important
Lives, souls, and spirits
Live
Love
And play

Until the day
Once
Young and foolish parents
Appear to say,

"Please,
Forgive us
For our thoughtless,
Selfish ways

Ways
Which haunt our nights
Ways
Which haunt our days"

He's dead
Pray he's alive
I don't know his name
She's dead

Pray she's alive
I don't know her name

I,
Alone,
As father,
Am to blame

The story in your palm
Is better left untold
Life is a curious journey
You can't GPS the road

Innocence
Can be
Destroyed
Like road kill under your wheels
You don't realize the damage
THEN

But,
One day,
You will feel
Sweet babe's breath
Like a whisper in the wind
Letting you know
What could
Or
Should have been

He dead
Pray he's alive
I don't know his name
She's dead
Pray she's alive
I don't know her name

I,
Alone,
As father,
Am to blame

BASE HEAD OF BROOKLYN

By Donald T. Williams

The Base Head of Brooklyn
Is who I once claimed to be
Crack smoking hippo
With a Master's Degree

Phatback Joe said my class
Was Krackology 101
Teacher, Donnie C's strict,
But his class was fun

Head of a classroom
Under the influence of drugs
Educated fool
And a lone wolf thug

Living oxymoron
Paradox in a suit
Made me feel uneasy
When Phatback Joe called me cute

Loving husband, breadwinner,
And a father of two
_____ didn't like it,
But what could she do?

Finally had enough
Walked the kids out the door
Knew she still loved me,
But couldn't—wouldn't take it no more

Left behind a page from a diary
Said she was up for anyone, anywhere
Prophetic words of anguish hurt so deeply,
But this man of dark secrets, as foretold, was prepared

Hurt and sacrifice
Would be the diet for all
My smoker's appetite
Could make the strongest man fall

What you folks don't know
Is that this inner conflict in me
Was part
Of a fortune telling mystery

Things a store front psychic
Years before had told me
Played out before my eyes
And these things fascinated greatly

Dealing with the occult
Or foreseers can be
More than tricky business
And living dangerously

PProphett 4 PProfitt
Donnie C has been called
Not a bit of this
Should I be telling you all

Sense I'm coming clean,
Want to fess up to all in a tale not tall?
Chips fall where they may!
Toss the coin, make a call!

Dealing with the Devil
Is no picnic or Ball
God has had my back
Picks me up when I fall

By the way, I do believe
God has sanctioned all of this
Loads my quiver with truth shots,
And Donnie C don't miss

TEACHERS

By Donald T. Williams

Teachers in the trench
Know well abuse's stinging stench
Cuts so deep, through bone to marrow
Still, they'll front the line today and tomorrow

With another day's lesson
Locked and loaded for the breach
A smart bomb, artillery shell, bunker buster
They hope and pray will reach

The "cute" little stick of dynamite
Wisecracking up
Like Clockwork Orange acting up
Every other day in the front, middle, or back seat

From the mouths of babes
Come words that truly dismay
How can teachers endure the pain
When what they teach is taught in vain?

Yet, the bright eyes laughing and impish smiles
Show true nature of the child
Much comfort teachers take in this
Seldom are the days they'll miss

To serve and teach as best as they can
The children who become men and women
Lovingly taught to raise their hands before they speak
And to meet our society's needs, rise to their peaks

Noble are the teachers' deeds,
And it hurts when students don't heed
Please, forgive any harsh words if heard abruptly said
Just recall the wonderful stories you and your teachers have read

Most have a moral lesson in them
Recall the places your imagination has been
Consider these poems you're reading an offbeat hymn
If you're really young, imagine the trouble you could be in

If you're really young, if by pure chance
This poetry has fallen in your hands
Get your parent's permission, dear child
Or take your chances young lady, young man

Look for life and English lessons taught
The Grey Spectre fishes for men, women, and children
If you continue reading,
Consider yourself caught

Teachers in the trench
Know well abuse's stinging stench
Cuts so deep, through bone to marrow
Still they'll front the line today and tomorrow

With another day's lesson
Locked and loaded for the breach
A smart bomb, artillery shell, bunker buster
They hope and pray will reach

DANCING ON RAINBOWS

BY Donald T. Williams

Ron Brown
Is no longer around
Flew up in a plane
That came crashing down

Left an impression
On many young Black men
You can run with or against the Whites,
But they're never your friend

They'll kill a plane load of "any" people
To get rid of "you"
Sky's the limit
When limiting, eliminating "you"

Now,
There's a Black man as President
Ron Brown must be proud
Dancing on rainbows
And skipping on clouds

Ron Brown did his part
To help pave the way
Ron Brown put in work
Back in the day

On Ron Brown's shoulders
Others have climbed
Now,
Ron Brown strolls
Streets of gold in Heaven
With the Devine

Ron Brown put in work
Back in the day

Sky walkers never let ceilings
Get in their way

In Brooklyn's
"Do or Die" Bed. Stuy.,
There was a school
In Ron Brown's name
The student's worked and played hard
Each day that they came

The sun often shined,
But some days it rained
If ever there was a loss,
It was found
And turned to a gain

Business as usual
Daily
Just be prepared
Ron Brown had worked hard
Ron Brown did his share

The teachers were flexible
Yet
Rigid as steel
Trained with much rigor,
But
They could feel

Love
For their students
Dedication
To their "chosen" careers
So much compassion
In their classrooms,
In their triumphs and tears

Now,
There's a Black man
As President
Ron Brown must be proud

71

Dancing on rainbows
And skipping on clouds

Ron Brown put in work
Back in the day
Sky walkers never let ceilings
Get in their way

Now,
It's your turn
To take to the skies
Keep your eyes on the ball
Keep your eyes on the prize

Who you trust
Is crucial too!
Trust in God
Only
It's personal,
The two of you

The sun often shines,
But some days it rains
If there's a loss,
Turn it to a gain

Ron Brown
Is no longer around
Flew up in a plane
That came crashing down

Yet,
Years later,
Tears later,
Cheers later

A Black man
Rose to the top
Some ceilings
Are
Very high

Some ceilings
Are
Dropped
Whatever sky
Lies above
Your beautiful mind
Get on top
Never let it stop

Helium filled,
Love filled
Balloons
Rise
With all they've got

Times
Appear to be changing
With the facade of change
A Black man
Won the Presidency
The "Race"
Considers this a gain

"Our"
Hopes are inflated
Like a "Village"
Of colorful, helium, love filled balloons

Raising
Rising aspirations
Of the "Village's" young and old
As high as the Sun at noon

Now,
There's a precedent
Ron Brown must be proud
Dancing on rainbows
And skipping on clouds

Now,
It's your turn

To take to the skies
Keep your eyes on the ball
Keep your eyes on the prize
All that glitters
Is not gold
Stratosphere status matters
As does your soul

We live in a country
Designed for "some" to get ahead
We live in a country
Where "some" desire God dead

In our rat race
Through the maze for cheese
Taking God out our lives
Hastens sin's disease

Stricken with a sickness
Passed on from birth
It takes a strong man or woman
To get to Heaven from earth

Money is the root of all evil,
But we all have to eat
An honest day's pay
For an honest day's work
Is all "honorable" persons seek

Having ambition alone
Won't get you safely through
You must have God
Inside of you

Who you trust
Is crucial too!
Just as important
As guess__?

Trust in God
Only
It's personal,
Just the two of you

HEY, MONROE

By Donald T. Williams

Hey, Monroe
Are you still there?

I never come see you
But know I still care

You were one of many
I failed to save

You and I slipped through the cracks
For our crimes, we have paid

Hey, Monroe
Why am I writing to you?

Perhaps there's still someway
I can help you?

I'll tell the world
I still think of you,

That I fell short
In self discipline,

That I fell short
In dedication, determination, and will

Just as you regret
The moment you killed

That I didn't live up to
What you deserved and expected from me

That I failed you, Monroe and more
Because of my hypocrisy

Hey, Monroe
By some chance, do you recall me,

And how our ships
Crossed by chance on life's stormy seas?

You were so young
In your early teens

You were so young
With a good heart and mind full of dreams

So much time has passed
Do you recall me?

Your "good intentions" teacher,
The one the children called Mr. DT?

I write to say
I still think of you

God
Has forgiven me,
And I know
God
Has forgiven you

Sarah Garnett,
MS 324
Has long since changed her name

Donald T. Williams

But
God
Loves
Her,
You,
And
Me
All the same

Hey, Monroe
Just had to let you know

SO YOU WILL KNOW

By Donald T. Williams

So you will know
And not forget
This is the Spirit
Of
Sarah Garnett

I
Roam
School halls

I
Roam
School rooms

Rising
All
Test levels
As hungry
Students consume

The daily food
Of
Lessons taught
Science and Math
Nutritious foods for thought

Reading and Writing
First,
Plant the seeds

That blossom as flowers
Even
Among the densest weeds

I
Am the spook
Who sat by the door

Challenging your minds:
Expand
And
Explore

The
UNIVERSE
That is your brain
VAST
Levels of knowledge,
RICHES
Unclaimed

I'm the spook
Making learning
A year round
Trick or Treat

The more
Problems you defeat
The more
Sweets of life you eat

If
By chance,
If
By pure happenstance,
If
By askance glance

One day,
You see
In misty vapors
The form
Of me

Don't be afraid
My darling child
'Twas Grey Spectre
Who asked that I

Briefly,
Give you sight of me
See the sight
Only
Believers,
Dream achievers see

Should we brush elbow
On an empty hallway pass,

Should you sense _____
When you complete a challenging task

Should you common sense the "good guess" and correct answer
Anticipate, before a question's asked

Should you seize a brain sifter concept
Only young Einstiens can grasp

'Twas your fate,
'Twas your destiny
To open your unique gifts
Only God
Could have given thee when conceived

So you will know
And not forget
This is the Spirit
Of
Sarah Garnett

I
Roam
School halls
I

Roam
School rooms

Rising
All test levels
As hungry students consume
The daily food
Of
Lessons taught
Science and Math,
High Proteins
For
Elevated Thought

Amplified
Reading and Writing
First,
Plant the crucial seeds

That blossom
As flowers,
Ascend
As trees
Even
Among weeds
Between windblown___'_____ seeds

So you will know
And not forget
This is the Spirit
Of
Sarah Garnett

I
Was
A
Principal,
A
Head
Of
School

I've long since passed
Yet,
I still pass through
Fulfill your destiny
Be not the fool

BEAT UP AND BUSTED

By Donald T. Williams

I was cracked up
I was angel dusted

I was buck wild
And could not be trusted

Oh no! Let me go!
Can't live this way no more

Living cracked up
Smoked up and hustling

What the fuck!
Make a buck!

It's my life!
Even if it sucks!

Soon I was torn up
She was busted

Oh no!
_____ a whore

Can't have
My love no more!

Shot down
To the ground

The bitch's bullets from a suppressed Silencer
Made no sound

But my will
She could not kill

Still standing, Solid Rock strong
As the Cing of the Hyll

Not some Sunken Ridge
Sinking in the sand,

Another Devil's Doorway
To the Nethermost Land

But don't feel abandoned
I'll be back for you

A "Man" never deserts his family
Don't expect me to

If it's all about riches,
Then let me shoot my load

Heaven's my House and my Bank
It's my humble abode; let all roll

Now I can chill
Who needs a mil?

I've billions to spare
Without a care

Don't mean to boast,
But did I dare say, "Billions to spare?"

All of them invisible, invincible,
Indispensible as clean air

God's blessings and forgiveness
Better than man's gold backed currency

ATM
Of loving care

Once I was beat up
I was busted

Can't be trusted
Living beat up

And busted
Can't be trusted

Hey, ___
You can rot!

Thought you
Were good as gold

Turns out
You're not!
You can pop and lock
Drop on the spot!

Know your XXX DVD was hot
Made your pimp (not you) a knot

If not,
You can still drop

Memories of you aren't gone;
Like a bad obsession, you ain't forgot

Tears like rain
Replenish flowers at a plot

Can you feel my tear drop,
You piece of snot?

Make the cash money rainmakers
Thunder and cheer

Make the cash splash
But don't drown in a sewer of hardcore moolah, liquor, and beer

It's pretty damn clear, my dear
You're a pretty, shitty smear, my dear

I was beat up
I was gut busted

Worse thing about it,
How can I doubt it?

Sweet Baby June
Was the one who couldn't be trusted

My ambitious now and forever ___
Was the one who was stone cold busted

But don't feel abandoned
I'll be back for you

A "Man" never deserts his family
Don't expect me to

PART TWO
PRIDE'S PRICE

IF FOR ME
DONNIE C's ENDS
DONNIE DON
IF I WIND UP DEAD
WHAT'S GOING TO HAPPEN?
DONNIE CAN'T LOSE

IF FOR ME

By Donald T. Williams

If for me, there is no peace
If for me, there is no relief
If all I have is pain and grief,
Then take my life without beef

Raise the white flag
Throw in the towel
Cut my torso
Disembowel

Living dead
Like some zombie beast
Still topside
But long deceased

It's no joke
This malignant condition
Cancerous growths
With no remission

When betrayed hearts
Are never fixed
Book passage
On the River Stix

An unearthly place
Is where I'm bound?
Do I smell the rot?
Do you hear the hounds?

My star crossed ex___
I'm sure to see?
Bound for the same
Hell as me?

Lord, have mercy
On our souls
Break the grip
Of Old Satan's hold

Playing games with God or the Devil
Ain't no fun and games
Either one's a big gamble
Winnings paid in pleasure or pain

DONNIE C's ENDS

By Donald T. Williams

Donnie C's simply out
To get his "Ends"
Donnie C wants to heal
Open wounds that won't mend

Donnie C has come face to face
With the Devil and some minions
Donnie C's going to see
This shit to the end

Troubles come and go
That's just a plain fact of life
Troubles come in doubles
When family and friends wield the knife

Aiming for your back
Just as the O'Jays have said
Niggers want to take you out
And leave you bleeding for dead

Yes, their wounds to me
Were deadly and deep
Thought they had me dead to rights
That's why I ain't heard from them a peep

Guess those sorry "family" niggers
Are waiting for Donnie C's other shoe to drop
One thing I can promise
Is that their bubble will loudly pop

Pop with the flare and fire
Of the Hindenburg balloon
Rain down hydrogen hell
Like a fiery monsoon

Donnie C's simply out
To get his "Ends"
Nigger don't give a fuck
Who he hurts or offends

Made your first mistake
When you fucked with his shit
Made your second mistake
When you thought Donnie C would stand for it

Made your third and last mistake
When you failed to put Donnie C down
Now Donnie C has risen
With a Kingly Crown

Gold, platinum, and diamonds
Don't rest on his head
His crown is the truth
In the poems you've read

Don't feel sorry for you
Really don't give a shit
Made yourself a target
And targets do get hit

Hope you've learned your lesson
Hope you've learned for sure
Bite back if you want to, Bitch
Donnie C has got plenty more

DONNIE DON

By Donald T. Williams

Donnie C
Knows he's not untouchable

Teflon Don
Donnie knows he is not

But his very name
Says Gangster

Even if he is a Don
Or even if he is not

Always been a hustler
When it comes to hard work, Donnie C isn't the least bit meek

Always working hard for others
And preferring to turn the other cheek

It's when you do something to him
Like a spiteful double and triple cross,

Some serious shit no one can like,
Have a blind eye, or eat a loss

Nigger won't stand for that sly, slick, sneaky shit
Works alone so spying eyes and lips can't trip and slip

But Donnie Don when he has to, he'll sanction work out
Call a "rain man" in the time of drought

Like Clint Eastwood on a Eiger Sanction hit
Handmade glove with a custom fit

So cold up on the mountain,
But a hired spitfire does bring the heat

Either way, you're going down,
Just a shot dead piece of meat

Like Ice Cube's Desolation Williams
Kicking ass in the Ghosts of Mars

Knock you out ice cold
Have you seeing stars

Donnie C
Knows he's not untouchable

Teflon Don
Donnie knows he is not

But his very name
Says Gangster

Even if he is a Don
Or even if he is not

Doing his best to avoid a life or death sentence
In a prison cell so dark and bleak

Ain't no punk, but he'll consider to turn his cheek
Before producing the smoking, hot heat

Will simmer for a time
Before he turns into a Beast,

The Beast which has always been in him
Lying dormant, trying to keep the peace

If his anger you awaken,
Even The Incredible Hulk will take a knee

Slaughter is as cattle
In a battle without victory

Donald T. Williams

All of us are a Two Face
Flipping a coin we know has two of the same sides

So Donnie C will hedge his bets
And Donnie C has been known to lie

Best you believe all of this shit though
It is as true as a true Robin's arrow and bow

You may change the channel,
Yet, wind up with another unreal, reality TV show

Donnie C is for real as is his appeal,
Upfront and with the real deal

Filling plates with truth
Like a buffet breakfast, lunch, and dinner meal

Donnie C
Knows he's not untouchable

Teflon Don
Donnie knows he is not

But his very name
Says Gangster

Even if he is a Don
Or even if he is not

Don't feel sorry for you
Really don't give a shit

Made yourself a target
And targets do get hit

IF I WIND UP DEAD

By Donald T. Williams

If I wind up dead
Before my natural days
If they find me
In some unnatural way

If I wind up missing
And can't be found at all
If I wind up rotting
In a jail cell so small

Take the word of Donnie C
It was a hit
Take the word of Donnie C
There's truth in his spit

Punk ass motherfuckers
Couldn't stand the diss dish I served
Punk ass motherfuckers
Didn't think I had the nerve

Well, my dumb ass niggers,
Gram and saltine crackers
Starved for creativity
Hard work slackers

You can choke on it
Savor every stroke of it
Never heard me tell you boys
To suck or fuck my dick

Donnie C's too much man
To "come" that way
Sorry, all my same sex homies or homos,
But there are some sick sex games I don't play

Now, don't be offended
Like some punk ass bitches
Crying in your beer
Because "your" biting and stealing made me riches

Tables turn on suckers, even cocksuckers
Each and every day
Merry Go Rounds go round and round the world
And everybody, even rough riders, must pay

Truth be told, the old shit you've made
Should or could be selling through the roof
Recycle those bad boys
Readers may want to hear for themselves, research the proof

Either way,
There's the Devil to pay
And finally there's God;
Wonder what He's going to say?

So laugh or cry
Over, at, or with Donnie C's goofs,
150 Spirited Proof,
Grey Spectre's white lightning crystal, serious spoofs

If I wind up dead
Before my natural days
If they find me
In some unnatural way

If I wind up missing
And can't be found at all
If I wind up rotting
In a jail cell so small

Take the word of Donnie C
It was a hit
Take the word of Donnie C
There's truth in his spit

WHAT'S GOING TO HAPPEN?

By Donald T. Williams

What's going to happen
To this troubled soul?
Donnie C wants to "get right"
Wants right to take firm hold

Donnie C's been writing
But his pen may dig a hole
Donnie C's going to write right
Writing right has been his goal
Donnie C writes with great might
What he writes comes from his soul

Donnie C not in a rush
To have more dirt thrown in his face
Donnie C not in a hurry
"The Big Sleep" can surely wait

Two Coins or is his name Two Quarters?
Told me I better "Get Right"
Ripped off my youngest __'_ skills and dough,
And that's more than just a slight

Small change motherfucker
So they shot your ass nine times
Only dumb ass niggers
Would send a hit man who's half blind

Phatback Joe said that all the summer
Will bring for me is death
Phatback Joe said that for the PProphett 4 PProfitt
What awaits is deep rest

Sorry to disappoint you
I'm sure you had "A View to a Kill"

Maybe I curved your bullet
Or the blind hit man can't shoot to kill

Sorry to disappoint you
Heard you declare, "Homie's going to die tonight"
Injection, lethal dose, or poison pill
Guess neither Kape Phear nor Brinn Marrs'
Doctor Death physicians could fill the bill or get the dosage right

Donnie C's going to keep on writing
Until his pens run out of ink
Donnie C's going to keep on writing
Until your shitty asses don't stink

Hope Roxxxy's black ass is still dancing
Crowds cloud burst dollars at her feet
Money does come sleazy
As does trouble with you creeps, the company she keeps

Hope her thong and high heels
Are still pink
Donnie C knows you niggers are still watching,
Waiting for Roxxxy's asshole to wink

What's going to happen
To this troubled soul?
Donnie C wants to "get right"
Wants right to take firm hold

Donnie C's been writing
But his pen may dig a hole
Donnie C's going to write right
Writing right has been his goal
Donnie C writes with great might
What he writes comes from his soul

Phatback Joe oinked,
"You in love with a stripper"
Phatback Joe belched,
"I fucked her and dissed her"

How'd she ever find his pinkie
Under all that slab?
Tiny pork sausage link
With pus and scabs

Ain't nothing pretty
About his ugly pink
Pig's penis in a blanket,
Wrapped in stink

Mystery solved concerning
Where those crabs came from
Knew damn well and for sure
That I wasn't the infested one

DONNIE CAN'T LOSE

By Donald T. Williams

Don't get angry
Don't get mad
Know you're gangsta
Know your fag swag

But with you
I got real beef
Ripped my goods
Like a damn thief

Trust my word
It's what I keep
Donnie C's reign his begun
Now I'm C and C

Don't expect mercy
Won't be no relief
Needless is the query,
"Where's the beef?"

Donnie C's a triple whopper
Topped with bacon and cheese
Donnie C's like McDonald's
Serving kids a Happy Meal

But, you thought Donnie
Was a Ronnie
And there may be
A bit of clown in me

But, when Donnie C. frowns,
It's as if the ground
Opened up and gave back
Emmet Kelly

It's like Jimi said,
"After all the Jacks
Have popped back in their boxes
And the clowns have all gone to bed"

Donnie C
Is still up laughing,
But the wind cries,
"Mary, his eyes are seeing red!"
"V" is for "Vendetta"
"V" is for "Victory" too!

Post them up together
And you get a "W"

"W" is for "Winner"
It's for my last name too!

And since Donnie C
Can't lose

Time you
Niggers,
Niggas,
And
Right Anglo crackers
Pay up
Ante up

Donnie C's
Ends,
Props,
And
Dues

PART THREE
VENUS' FLYTRAP

HOW MUCH?
I AM A BEAST!
THIS SHIT
NOSEY MOTHERFUCKERS
SUNKEN RIDGE
HOOKER HAT
BEE AND ME
MY PRIME RIB
ALPHA BETA SOUP
DR. LIVINGSCUM, I PRESUME?
SMALL TOWN

HOW MUCH?

By Donald T. Williams

How much is a man
Supposed to take
Before a man
Retaliates?

Heard a man without a gun
Is not a man
Just a sitting duck down range
Of "The Man" who can

Pull the lip trigger
Most deftly
As lucid
As "fluid"
As a "dope" rapper's injection
On the mike
Or "flow"
As a fine thespian,
Big or small screen
Sensational sight

Heard a man is a man
If he can quell his rage
Hear or read
What bad is spoken
Or
Written about him
And
Simply turn the page

Let it roll off him
Like a duck or a Teflon Don
Trash talking mudslingers
Are the pigs of the farm

Trash talking people
Try,
But in my case,
Do no harm
Dapper Teflon Dons
Ooze too much charm

Heard a strong chin
Can take a few blows and keep blowing
Many men down his throat
Both cheeks broken and swollen

Firsthand knowledge,
I'll never have
Take thrice as many with me
As you savages have or would have

You came for me once,
And you will come again,
But this man won't go quietly,
Raise as much __ as I can

Combine the tornadoes' spins
Hurricanes',
Blizzards'
Monsoons'
Siroccos',
And
Volcanic
Eruptions'
Winds

Last man
Or
Thing standing
Won't be you
Or
Yours

Got
"Passover"

All over me,
My, mines
And
All "our" doors

Crimes
Against nature
Same as crimes
Against God and me
Take aim at Him or me
The target you be
See?

Rolling thunder will not cease
Lightning flashes multiply their increase
Rivers raging overflow their banks
Ships,
Once floats,
Will now sink as tanks

Firsthand knowledge
Do I have?
Life preservers thrown,
But who will grab?

How much is a man
Supposed to take
Before a man
No longer hesitates?

How much is a man
Supposed to take
Before a man
Retaliates?

Heard a man without a gun
Is not a man
Just a sitting duck down range
Of "The Man" who can

Yet,
Even bigger caliber,
Natural disaster guns
Are trained on you,
And what's received
Measures much more
Than thrice what's due

Overkill
Is how it's known
Perhaps,
You should leave a "Man" alone?

Senseless babble
Of an unknown poet,
Plenty of stones on the ground
Why don't you throw it?

I AM A BEAST!

By Donald T. Williams

This is the story
I must tell

Thought I knew you
And knew you well

I'm a teacher
So I must teach

I have sound lessons
And people I must reach

But for you, my ex honey,
Class time has run out

The final bell has rung
And there is no doubt

For you,
I now care the least

For you,
Consider me a most savage beast

For you,
The Mission Bell will not ring
For you,
The Hounds of Hell will sing

Bite, slash, and tear
At your once sweet derriere

It's what you should get
It's only fair

For a shark like you,
I was fresh fish bait on a hook

For a slimy, slippery eel like you
I should have seen your snake like looks

My love was blind
To the subtlety of your cruelty

So blind to the reality
Of love's liability

That you'd abuse my love,
My absolute trust in you

I was a fool for your love
You knew it true!

That you used your conditional love
To take advantage of me

That you abused my love
As others abused thee sadistically

Viciously,
For the weird, wicked world to see

Time has come for Donnie C, the teacher
To take you to school

Time for Donnie C, the teacher
To find his ruler and lose his cool

You might have thrown me to the curb
Out in the street, or down a ditch

You might have told me I was homeless,
"So, go to "no home", bitch."

You might have shot me full of holes,
But your spitfire barrage has missed

111

Donnie C's here to say
There's no way

That in his presence
You will exist

School is completely out for you
There's not a damn thing you can do

Donnie C says you're dismissed
You don't exist when me you dissed

Hear me, Mrs.
You are dismissed

If _____
Is what you wish

Then please, take everything,
Including your diss

I am a Beast
To anyone who fucks with me!

I am a Beast
Lion, Alien, Predator, Terminator, Cloverdale BEAST!

I am a Beast
Day the Earth Stood Still Monster Robot, programmed to kill to
keep the peace!

Who else wants to fuck with Donnie C?
Who else loves a page turning mystery?

Thumb the pages from back to front
Read the lines between the font

History repeats itself
Speaks and reeks most candid and blunt

Regurgitated, tell tale heart pumps
Stinks like an angry, dead skunk

But it's best uncovered
No dust jacket suits this "black tie" tale

That pains as if cuticle
Torn from a tender fingernail

THIS SHIT

By Donald T. Williams

If this shit began
In the December of 2006

You're probably wondering,
"Why I'm bringing up this old shit?"

I bring it up because this old bullshit
Can't seem to leave me alone

Try hard not to think of it,
But these memories still live on

Memories of a family
That I once had

Memories of a happy _____
That eventually went bad

Thought I had a life
And future on Easy Street

Worked hard all my life
And retirement looked sweet

Stepped right in some bullshit
My bitch ___ set in my way

Think she laid the shit herself
Because it sure seemed that way

Loved her so
She's good as gold

Somehow believed
That her shit didn't stink

Until I caught her
In the pink

Making her tight
Asshole wink

Turns out this slimy bitch
Had done me grimy for years
Fronting like a good ___
And ___ of my two ___

Principal by day,
And some pimp's bitch on the side

Caught her in a Triple X
While some honky rebel busted her black ass wide

Screaming like a child
Who never had it at the backdoor

Shaking, crying tears
She screamed her head off for More, More, More!

That's what I would say
Would be the start of this shit

Really should be 2003, at the Summer Picnic,
But I won't knit pick

BBackk Street Hooker, BBlackk Street Hookers
Roxxxy Raynalds is her screen you might say

See if you can find a copy;
Give it a play

20 million copies sold
Or so brags CraZy

Donald T. Williams

Heard he sold them out of his car trunk
Never said this nigger was LaZy

20 million copies sold
You probably already have yours

Watched it 20 million times
And never got bored

Hope both your hands aren't tired
Given all the time that's been spent

Run out and buy a sadistic friend a copy
CraZy must pay his and that bitch Bee's rent

Don't feel sorry for you
Really don't give a shit
Made yourself a target
And targets do get hit

Bull's eye like an asshole
Donnie C's bullets fly straight or curve

Your dumbass went and did it
Where did you get the nerve?

Now, I'm sticking justice
Where it can't be left behind

That light at the end of the tunnel
Is the diamond in the mind

It may take some effort
To pass this precious stone

Grey Spectre digs ever deeper
Such diamonds are never alone

NOSEY MOTHERFUCKERS

By Donald T. Williams

How would you
Feel if perfect strangers knew everything about you?

How would you
Feel if they were observing everything you do?

Following you throughout the streets
Everywhere you go, there are some of those creeps

Watching you and filming
For some clandestine TV show

You catch some late night TV
And watch a parody of you unfold

Object of their amusement,
Their Simple Simon clown

Invasion of my privacy
Would make me feel so down

Truman Show is how they played me
Only this intrusion was much too real

Saw you in the Post Office, the DMV, CVS,
Greene Ford, and at the mall

Saw you at Blockbuster, the movie theater, Circuit City,
Golden Corral, Red Lobster, and that's not all

Scoped you so many places
My skin literally began to crawl

Donald T. Williams

When motherfuckers constantly stalk you,
This big world becomes quite small

But I just went with it,
I was curious to know

Who are these nosey ass motherfuckers?
What's their motive? How elaborate is this web I'd like to know?

Delusional motherfucker's mind fucked
From so much crack
Think what you like home invaders,
But Donnie C is nothing like that

Donnie C just played along
Gave you plenty of returns

The more you kept coming back
The more of you I learned

Mugged for the camera
Gave you assholes a prime time show

Just to see how far
You sons of bitches would go

Must admit, you saw me
Get away with some off the chain shit

Only thing wrong
With this back and forth game of ping pong

Was that I knew someone, besides me
Was mysterious, curious, and delirious with glee

Was getting a bigger kick
And loving every bit

Watching me get away with
Some off the chain shit

Didn't like you parked outside my crib,
Coming in and wearing my fine clothes

Didn't like you dressing like me,
Trying to hijack my ID

Why you motherfuckers
Biting off Donnie C?

Bunch of dumbass motherfuckers
Want to be like me; now "that's" a mystery!

Bunch of hustler motherfuckers
Out to rip off my shit

In and out my "private" home,
Leaving your unflushed shit

Warm hamburgers left behind on the counter,
And I've been gone for over six hours

Making fuck films in my crib
Whenever I'm locked up, committed, or gone long enough for
fresh milk to sour

Did you think that Donnie C
Didn't see you sons of bitches?

Donnie C was taking notes,
Halfheartedly laughing; holding side splitting stitches

Knowing damn well,
Any teacher, crack head, or rocket scientist could tell

These dastardly deeds
Took leafy green backing, planning, conspiracy, and cruel crafting as well

Nosey motherfuckers had me in straight faced stitches,
But I've got something for you, bitches

119

Donald T. Williams

You motherfuckers "know" Donnie C
"Did" tell you straight up

I'll start _____ the domes from under those ballpark caps
And not give a New York Yankee fuck

Global warfare what's you want?
Well suckers, that's what you got

Standing tall
Or stooping low

There's no getting around
The microwave's flow

Your nosey asses
Like hot, buttered, kernels

Will feel the vibes,
The heat internal

You're going to get popped,
10.0
Before and Aftershock

Donnie C don't give a fuck,
And you can believe that he don't

If Donnie C says "Fuck you!"
There's no way that he won't

This old school motherfucker
Will chalk dust your ass

Literally, bust your ass
Like an immortal, moral episode of Gunsmoke

Terminator,
Detonator,
Heat Seeker,
Remote Grim Reaper

Or
Soul Redeemer
Most certain and for sure

Donnie C's literary warhead
Will
Persuade
Or
Nuke
All
On every land and every shore

Always been a writer
Without a story to tell

Now,
Jet fuel's on this Trufiction
So,
It's going to scorch like Hell

Don't worry about the pulp or Kindle
As long as you love to read

Donnie C's teaching a moral lesson
Let me know if I did or didn't succeed

SUNKEN RIDGE

By Donald T. Williams

What about those 06' slayings
In lovely Sunken Ridge,
Beautiful subdivision in the Sand Hills
Where I used to live?

For all appearance's sake
The people and homes appear safe,
But I believe the new I-295
Brought murderers out for a drive

Getting off I-95
They'd kick it for a while
Ride through subdivisions
And put an unlikely household through trials

Seems I heard a Phatback Joe rapper
Shot calling and bragging about some "drama" like this
Stupid authorities surely missed it,
But I'm onto this home invasion shit

When it comes to murder,
Fayfartville Sheriffs are Keystone Cops
Only good for Black man harassment, arrests,
And bullshit traffic stops

A mother and two children
Found dead in their "safe" home
Somehow their restless spirits
Won't leave me alone

Will never get used to triple killings
Right in my backyard

Have you Fayfartville Keystones solved those terrible, triple
murders,
Or is that too hard?

Inbred bastards and bitches
Aren't too smart
For the most part,
Tenderfoot tards with the inflated egos of gun toting Security
Guards

Yet, for them, there's always a beat on the street
Job security and all that
But if these murders have still gone unsolved,
Then I smell an "inept" rat pack
Rats with uniforms
Rats with guns
Rats who failed
The murdered ones

False accusations!
What's the truth?
Keystone Cops of Fayfartville
Can't find the proof

What about those 06' slayings
In lovely Sunken Ridge,
Beautiful subdivision in the Sand Hills
Where I used to live?

Time to warm this cold case up
Serve the facts and forensics hot on a plate
Keystones may have swept it under the rug,
But uncovering the truth is never too late

A mother and two children
Found dead in their "safe" home
Somehow their restless spirits
Won't leave me alone

Will never get used to triple killings
Right in my backyard

Donald T. Williams

Have you Fayfartville Keystones solved those terrible, triple
murders,
Or is that too hard?

Seems I heard a Phatback Joe rapper
Shot calling and bragging about some "drama" like this
Stupid authorities surely missed it,
But I'm onto this home invasion shit

Motherfucker talking about "I run this shit,
And you ain't eating here!"
You might have fucked that bitch,
But I ain't got no fear

I left on my own
In the midst of a circumstance
In which I knew "I" was wrong
It was an in house,
Family matter
Smog, you're smoking your own rocks
If you think "you" made be scatter
Next,
I hear you talking flagrant shit
I
Interpret,
Analyze,
And
Scrutinize
Every shitty bit
In a CD of "fair to middlin" piece of crap rap songs

Got your big,
Pig head
Stuck and star struck
In my business
Like a Phat Head wall poster
Where it doesn't belong

Yeah,
I can see why it took you ten years
To write your mother some heartfelt bullshit

124

Had to bit off MJ
So,
We all know how you rip

I don't listen to much rap,
Butt,
You're a two-bit,
One hit wonder,
Without a true gift

What about those 06' slayings
In lovely Sunken Ridge,
Beautiful subdivision in the Sand Hills
Where I used to live?

Any answers for a crazy crack head,
Any justice for the innocent and the dead,
Is all this shit just delusions of a basket case,
Or is there truth in what I've said?

What about those 06' slayings
In lovely Sunken Ridge,
Beautiful subdivision in the Sand Hills
Where I used to live?

HOOKER HAT

By Donald T. Williams

Honey bun of mine
In a Cowgirl Hooker Hat
Off to Atlanta, GA
Like an "in heat" alley cat

Pretense for the trip
So dubious and ill-conceived
I felt the need
To hurl and grieve

Trusting me,
My blind love
Couldn't see

Let home girl go
Freely,
Out the door
From that day on
She was mine no more

Months later,
Here's a Dear John Birthday Card
Putting two and two together
For me is not hard

I believe in plenty
Of hope and rope
Give a fine niggress,
Like a castle tower bound Princess,
Plenty rope and hope

More than enough lifeline,
The length of the longest vine,

To hang free,
To swing over the moat

But never let someone dock,
Never float another's boat
Because then she could and should
Choke at the end of her rope

Lady's now a tramp
What's a _____ to do?
___ beat her shirt would never fit me,
And my love is still true

True,
I've done my dirt
Now,
What comes around
Has gone around,
Only to return
As a lonely sum

Our numbers were four,
But
I have been reduced to minus one

Honey bun of mine
In a Cowgirl Hooker Hat
More Coyote Ugly Cougar,
I have never seen
Wake me from this nightmare
Who has stolen my dream?

What I say next
May sound further
Than far-fetched,
But
I'll still cast the net,
And
See what I catch

I believe
In plenty of rope
And you best believe,
Donnie C is no joke

Honey bun of mine
In a Cowgirl Hooker Hat
Lady's now a tramp
Like an "in heat" alley cat

Saw a bullet hole in a hat like it
Somebody's dome got capped
Saw home girl with an "obviously" different face
And wondered why she looked like that?

Got a glimpse of JB
Clowning and wearing a "similar" hat in Jett
Sounds improbable, confusing, and crazy,
But I made the connect

Didn't JB
Die on a '06 Christmas Day?
Sure took an awfully long time
To put JB away

Big star like the GF of S
Had to receive his props,
And his head was hard,
But the bullet was stopped

Chuck the close-up Mr. DeMille,
Close the casket, and read the will
Did JB die on a '06 Christmas Day?
Sure took a long time to put JB away

Sure am glad
I stopped smoking crack
This story is "more than strange" without a pipe load
And downright "whacked"

Motherfucking pigs had me locked up
For thirteen days
At the same time to be exact
That's another "Too much of a coincidence",
Another "What the fuck?" fact

Honey bun of mine
In a Cowgirl Hooker Hat
Off to Atlanta, GA
Like an "in heat" alley cat

Pretense for the trip
So dubious and ill-conceived
I felt the need
To hurl and grieve

Too active an imagination,
Too many drugs,
Too many senseless lamentations
Beating a dead horse like a rug?

One,
Some,
All,
Or
None
Of the above,
Poor bastard should end his misery,
Empty a full clip of slugs?

Fucked up personal history
And
Really,
Who cares?
Now,
The nigger's out to save or slay the world
With a mouthful of curses and lip service prayers

Take the loss
Tear up the I O U's
Protect your ___
At all cost to you

Man, this sordid tale
Could go on and on
Either way,
As a man, be strong

Tell me,
Has the best of chivalry
Been laid to rest?
Seems women have our rib,
But crave all of the rest

Man, this sordid tale
Could go on and on
Either way,
As a man, be strong

Honey bun of mine
In a Cowgirl Hooker Hat
Off to Atlanta, GA
Like an "in heat" alley cat

No longer around
To scratch my back
Give anything
To win her back

BEE AND ME

By Donald T. Williams

Ring the alarm
Donnie C is the bomb
Blasting cities to farms
With his words, wit, and charm

So, you want to upgrade me?
Like my barber who fades me?
True, once I leave his chair
People stop, look, and stare

Bee, can you do the same?
Make the leopard's spots change?
Deal with DC restrained
Or unleash the untamed?

Could it be, just may be
It's the spirit in me?
Just as plain as can be
No more crack head they see

The Grey Spectre is loose
Giving egos a bruise or a boost
Golden eggs laid the goose
Twenty four karat proof

When I hear your 06' songs
They ring true and never wrong
Kevin Krisp Bacon and his six degrees
Connected us oh so mysteriously

Slowly, as the earth rotates
Paths do cross by twists of fate
Remember the Jacksonville, NC bus stop over four years ago?
You there, disguised like a home girl, incognito

Donald T. Williams

When our eyes met
You knew I knew
Your "cover" was blown
But I smiled and ignored you

Next, your Bee Dae CD songs
Flaunt an insight of my life
I don't know you,
But do you know my ___?

Stuff I'm hearing lately
A third party should not know
Am I being made a fool of?
Am I a clown in a clandestine circus show?

Ring the alarm
Donnie C is the bomb
Blasting cities to farms
With his words, wit, and charm

So, you want to upgrade me?
Like my barber who fades me?
True, once I leave his chair
People stop, look, and stare

Bee, can you do the same?
Make the leopard's spots change?
Deal with DC restrained
Or unleash the untamed

Could it be, just may be
It's the spirit in me?
Just as plain as can be
No more crack head they see

The Grey Spectre is loose
Giving egos a bruise or a boost
Golden eggs laid the goose
Twenty four karat proof

MY PRIME RIB

By Donald T. Williams

Pray you had nothing
To do with the crime
Pray you had nothing
To do with stealing my prime

Rib,
Corresponding part of me
___,
To whom I gave heart freely

If you did nothing,
Were not involved,
Then you owe nothing
And are absolved

Say you're proud
Of what you did
Fear not man's jails
Or the long term bid

Say you don't pray
Then to Hell with you,
But before you go
Pay your I.O.U.

Pay in full
"Before" I forgive your unscrupulous ass
Take the bull by the horns
For I will not ask

The reason why
Which I know was cash
The reason why
I will not look past

An eye for an eye
Come up with my dough
An eye for an eye
There's no love any mo'!

Perhaps it's lost
And can't be found
Must be so
Neither you nor love comes around
Say you're proud
Of what you did,
Say what you took
Was the Devil's to give?

Things of this world
Will slip through our hands
None is worse off
Than the sinful man

Firsthand knowledge
From which I speak
Now testifies
That all sin is weak

Feeble
Compared to God's awesome wrath
Powers
He wields
Will execute the task
Ridding the world
Of its sinful scum
"You'll be paid in full;
We'll have won

God
Fights all my battles
Lord
Sets my daily course
Holy Spirit
Speaks to me

Verses written,
His discourse

Pray
You had nothing
To do with the crime
Pray
You had nothing
To do with stealing my prime

Rib,
Corresponding part of me
——,
To whom I gave my heart,
My love freely

ALPHA BETA SOUP

By Donald T. Williams

Delltah is the fourth letter
In a Greek alphabet soup
Delltah is a love triangle
In which the _____ gets duped

Delltah is the bloody deposit
At a dead red river's mouth
Delltah is the betrayal
Of an evil ___ of her love struck _____

Sorry, sorority sisters
All decked out in red
Bloodstained menstrual cycles
Monthly soil their expensive threads

Try and fail to clean them up
In white dresses they're so sweet!
Bitter dark chocolate melts in the mouths
Of tobacco chewing, redneck creeps

Pick them out like broncos
To be ass broken whores
Pry open their bottoms
With a crowbar that's raw

Yet, they prance around the dance
All those Fillies in heat
Young and old slavish whores do their chores
And the dirty deeds most discrete

At conferences
At seminars
Gather
The "respectable" crude

Pay homage
To the Devil himself
And mix
In an orgy's stew

Once upon a time on TV, I witnessed pleasure's misery
Saw two rednecks describe
How a fine married mare
Was "cut from the herd for a specific ride"

How they "broke" a new whore
Skillfully, slipped a German Unit up her back
And bid her to beg, in fact
To scream and cry out for more, more, more

Wild Willie Idoll sang about it
In one of his greatest songs
Rebel rode her mule ass
Broke her so wildly and so wrong for so long

Saw the same honkies brag brazenly
About such a "sight" never before seen
True, I haven't had a restful night yet
Without seeing and hearing how she screamed, screamed, and
screamed

Maybe, if I write about it,
I can put this nightmare to rest
Meanwhile, millions watch the XXX DVD again and again
To see Roxxxy, an undressed, dehumanized mess

Delltah is the fourth letter
In a Greek alphabet soup
Delltah is a love triangle
In which the _____ gets duped

Delltah is a bloody deposit
At a dead red river's mouth
Delltah is a betrayal
Of an evil ___ of her love struck sponge

Donald T. Williams

Sorry, sorority sisters
All decked out in red
Bloodstained menstrual cycles
Soil even the old bitches' expensive treads

Try and fail to clean them up
In white dresses they're so sweet!
Bitter dark chocolate melts in the mouths
Of tobacco chewing, redneck creeps

Pick them out like broncos
To be ass broken whores
Pry open their bottoms
With a crowbar that's raw

Yet, they prance around the dance
All those Fillies in heat
Young and old slavish whores do their chores
And the dirty deeds most discrete

At conferences
At seminars
Gather
The "respectable" crude

Pay homage
To the Devil himself
And mix
In an orgy's stew

Delltah is the fourth letter
In a Greek alphabet soup
Delltah is a love triangle
In which a loving _____ gets duped and his _____ droops

Elephant trunks resemble symbols
Snouts up all through the house
All walls nix the Crucifix
What's that all about?

Everywhere you look
There's another elephant figurine

So many phalluses in the crib
Baby girl, it's obscene

Heard each one's a trophy
Memory of some well hung fraternity man
Sorry sorority sisters really live it up
You go girl! Ain't life grand!

Rednecks got so much money and power
And nothing else to do
But take hardworking people to play with
And make a Black man look like a fool

News flash, motherfuckers
Hope you can give as well as you take
I'm coming with the
Crowbar
Jack hammer
Chisel
Pick ax
Shovel
Backhoe
Pile driver
Pneumatics, dynamite, nitro,
And mountain leveling earthquakes

About to tear you a "new one"
Call it "a gruesome screw some for one", scum
And you know how it's done
So, for you this won't be fun

And let there be no mistake,
I'm about to bust your ass legally
So please,
Don't call it rape

At conferences
At seminars
Gather round
The "respectable dude"

Pay homage to the Father, the Son, and the Holy Spirit
To Donnie C
And mix
In Grey Spectre's soup, coupe, brew, or crew

Four sided triangles
Can they possibly exist?
Diagonals in a square
Are they proof of this?

Delltah is the fourth letter
In a Greek alphabet soup
Delltah is a four sided love triangle
In which a duped _____ recoups

Small fortunes gained
Greater fortunes lost
Defiled and shamed
Won't you come to the Cross?

DR. LIVINGSCUM, I PRESUME?

By Donald T. Williams

Which doctor
Do you trust with your life?
Which doctor
Do you trust with your ___?

Time for another colonoscopy
No wonder who is up for the job
Dr. Livingscum, I do presume
Uses fingers like a sexual rod

Size really doesn't matter
Once in his skillful hands
Probes up to his elbows
All patients think Doc's grand!

Yes, they sing his praises
Each and every one
Farts remind them of him
Bowel movements leave them stunned

Such a voodoo doctor!
This nigger's way on the other side of town,
Butt in their minds he's with them
Every time a colon clearing, shit storm dumps down

I'll never get this treatment
I'll go out "backed up" like John Wayne
If prunes don't clear the plumbing,
Then extra effort on the abdominal strain

Never in Dr. Livingscum's hands
Will you ever find my cheeks
Day I met that motherfucker
I knew he was a creep

____ used to "love" him
Now, I know why and understand
'Twas what his fingers could do
In and out a can

Time for another colonoscopy
No wonder who is up for the job
Dr. Livingscum, I do presume
Uses fingers like a sexual rod

Which doctor has the magic touch?
Which doctor has a way, "his way" with butts?
Which doctor leaves your colon clean?
Which doctor comes with you in wet dreams?

Such a voodoo doctor!
This nigger's way on the other side of town,
Butt in their minds he's with them
Every time a colon clearing, shit storm dumps down

Size really does matter
Once in his skillful hands
Probes up to his elbows
All patients think Doc's grand!

Yes, they sing his praises
Each and every one
Farts remind them of him
Bowel movements leave them stunned

____ used to "love" him
Now, I know why and understand
'Twas what his fingers could do
In and out a can

SMALL TOWN

by Donald T. Williams

Redd Slimy Spwrings is a small town
Place to be ignored
Birthplace of my evil ___
Burial ground for that whore

Knew that she was country,
But in the city, grew up fast
Now _____ a "big" porn star
Making money shaking that ass

Shake what your Momma gave you
May that cockeyed tollbooth rest in peace
Please don't be offended y'all
It's "all good" to say the least about your deceased

Redd Slimy Spwring is a red wine Kotex
Full of White trash, niggers, niggas
And "wannabe" Indian Chiefs
Most of them on
Welfare,
Weed,
Beer,
Liquor,
Crack,
Or
Meth
There are numerous forms of relief

True,
I spent some time there
It was second home to me
Now,
It's just a bloody rag
There are no fond memories

Donald T. Williams

Hope you niggers are still cracking,
Frying fish, and telling jokes
Watch out for the bones though;
Donnie C wants y'all niggers to choke

Redd Slimy Spwrings is a small town
Place to be ignored
Birthplace of my evil ___
Burial ground for that whore

PART FOUR
VERBAL BARRAGE

COVER YOUR EARS, CLOSE YOUR MOUTH
DON'T FEEL SORRY
WELL-DESERVED
NIGGER SAID
SWINE ON THE MIKE
FYI
PIMP'S WOE
MOSQUITOES AND GNATS
GO TO SLEEP MAGGIE
WHAT'S UP WITH
ON THE HOOK
PROBLEM REVOLVER
YEAH, YOU HEARD RIGHT

COVER YOUR EARS, CLOSE YOUR MOUTH

By Donald T. Williams

I know you're out there,
Motherfucker

I know you're out there,
Bitch

I'm calling you,
Motherfucker

And I'm calling you,
Bitch

I'm calling,
Motherfucker

I'm calling,
Motherfucking Bitch

And I'm calling,
Mother
Fucking
Sons
Of
A
Bitch!

Get your Judas asses
Over here, Motherfuckers!

Get your punk, Brutus asses over here
My ___ of a bitch!

Sold me out,
The embarrassing _____

Three stabs in my back
Could not have been any harder,

But I'm a resurrection
Standing tall, erect, and correct

Setting out to kill me
Was a triple negative

With a positive, XXX
Cause and effect

Come to Pappa!
Don't let that bitch stop ya!

Act like men
Break away from that Mother Hen

Unless on the chopping block,
She's got you by the throat

Then, like her, there's no fixing you
Your asses and necks are forever broke

I know you're out there,
Motherfucker

I know you're out there,
Bitch

I'm calling you,
Motherfucker

And I'm calling you,
Bitch

I'm a disgusted,
Curse busting,

Diss thrusting,
Offended avenger

My "Super" Supernatural blast,
The best offer I'll entreat

Come;
Get trapped in Grey Spectre's Moral Pollution Solution Trash
Talking Crap Trap;
Be forever scrapped and wrapped at the bottom of the High
Treason Heap

It's where you belong
RIP

Don't feel sorry for you
Really don't give a shit

Made yourself a target
And targets do get hit

DON'T FEEL SORRY

By Donald T. Williams

Don't feel sorry for you
Really don't give a shit
Made yourself a target
And targets do get hit

Heard vengeance is a death dish
Served best when it's served cold
Mine has marinated
In a freezer's Sub Zero cold

Just like 007
You'll come to know my name
Just like 007
The coldest blood runs through my veins

Take Donnie C seriously
He's not shaken,
And
He's not stirred
Aston Martin lightening fast
When I pass,
I'm just a blur

You'll be playing catch up
From now to the end of time
Can't wait for your rebuttal
Can't wait for your end rhyme

You will never come
Up with an answer to all this
Shoot back if you see me,
But watch out, I'll make you miss

You see,

I've got the power
To make your bullets curve
You see,
I've got the power
To strip you of your nerve

Don't feel sorry for you
Really don't give a shit
You're the ones who started it,
But I bet I make you quit
Sit and roll over
Like a dog
Trained
To do tricks

Have your head
In your lap
Taking get clean
Nasty licks

Don't feel sorry for you
Really don't give a shit
Better be
More careful
With the fights
You chose to pick

Don't feel sorry for you
Really don't give a shit
Made yourself a target
And targets do get hit

When it's all said
And done,
"You Only Live Twice",
Mr. Don

Donnie C
Should be
Very rich
Ain't that a bitch!

Donald T. Williams

A husband,
A father,
A teacher,
A crack head

Niggers,
Crackers,
Dealers,
Hustlers,
And
Pimps
Can't trick!

Saints,
Ain't that a____?

WELL-DESERVED

By Donald T. Williams

Silence is the pounding
Ringing in my ear
Solitude is the substance
That brings one eye to tear

Lonely is the island
Remote and far away
Victim is the mild child
Who at recess is the bullies' play and prey

Smoldering are embers
In a fire that won't die
Memories of the wrongs endured
Make red the eye-for-an-eye

For those who have it coming
Your future is your past
You'll know who pulled the _____
No guess or need to ask

___ are Equalizers
When you walk these streets alone
Confirmed kills waiting to happen
Personally impersonal as drones

First,
Cheap wine shared with buddies
Delays the time a life you'll take
Second,
Reefer provides a smokescreen
Puts on a smile and quells the hate

Small arms reassure you
"That the next time, I'll be damned"

Dare not lay hand upon me
Be you woman, child, or man

Hood code grown to live by
Because this lone wolf stalks alone
And Mommy always told me
That the gallows will take me home

So,
Street drugs eased the pressure
Of loathing, self-prophecy, and fate
Workaholic ethics
Kept shelter, clothing, and food on my plate

___ ___ ___ made a family
But were they ever really mine?
Truth came out in the long run,
And how they did me was a crime

Things are of no company
For the company now lost
This gypsy roams with a facsimile home,
A rolling stone absent of moss

Aging hippie with no drugs or sex
Makes rock-n-roll a bore
Teenage spirit rots with age
When a ___ "turns out" as whore

When she sets you up as "chump,"
She and her "close circle of friends"
Money is the root of all evil
And adultery is a sin

Phatback Joe from the Bronx
Said, "There's no fixing them"
Once the German Unit busts that ass
Saw it myself on a triple X DVD
And word,
That shit drilling was crass

A conspiracy so elaborate
I have to tell this tale
May have happened years ago,
But this story's far from stale

Smoldering are embers
In a fire that won't die
Memories of the wrongs done
Make red the eye-for-an-eye

Hood code grown to live by
Because this lone wolf stalks alone
And Mommy always told me
That the gallows will take me home
Think I'm talking bullshit,
Exhaled excrement
Passed as a crack head's gas in vaporous pipedream?
Imagine yourself screaming
The way that banshee ___ screamed

"That"
Will
"Never"
Go down easy
As in a virgin,
Untapped ass
What I saw was monstrous,
And I will "never" let it pass

Never forgive
Never forget
My "circle of foes"
Well-deserved
What they'll get

For those who have it coming
Your future is your past
You'll know who pulled the _____
No guess or need to ask

Same way you got to know me
I,
In turn,
Will get to know you
Now Donnie C's doing the plotting and stalking
As verses do the talking and walking too

All you well-known "stars"
Donnie C. knows "exactly" who you are
Fans may worship near and far,
But I know the "scum" you are

Never forgive
Never forget
My "circle of foes"
Well-deserved what they'll get

Silence is the pounding
Ringing in my ear
Solitude is the substance
That brings one eye to tear
Lonely is the island
Remote and far away
Victim is the predator
And numbered are your days

Smoldering are embers
In a fire that won't die
Memories of the wrongs endured
Make red the eye-for-eye

For those who have it coming
Your future is your past
You'll know who pulled the _____
No guess or need to ask

Never forgive
Never forget
Well-deserved
What they'll get

My "circle of foes"
Experience
Extreme woes
Their future forebodes

Misfortunes
Promised
As cruelty
In kind

Wine
Sweet and aromatic
Vinegar
Impure and sour
Fruits
Of the same vine

Fruits
Of my labor
Will make them regret
Well-deserved
What they'll get

NIGGER SAID

By Donald T. Williams

Nigger said,
Motherfucker, you ain't shit!

Nigger said,
Motherfucker, suck my dick!

Nigger said,
Sucker, your ____'_ a whore!

Nigger said,
Fool, that bitch loves me more!

Nigger said,
Homie, your ___'_ also my bitch!

Nigger said,
Your brains and rhymes have made me rich!

Well, Donnie C's here
To let you niggers know
Bitch ass motherfuckers,
For now, you can keep that whore
____ did me grimy
I may love but can't want her no more!

Tossed me to the curb
Next to a pile of shit
Picked myself up, got clean,
And now I'm over it a bit, but here's the hitch,

One thing I "must have"
And I "will take" my dues,
Mounting and counting mountain stacks of cheese
In this entertainment game just like you

Difference is I'm a man
A rhyme slinger, rap star wringer, humdinger too
More MAN
Than sorry, low, rainmaking niggers like you

Pimp,
Gangster,
Thug,
Dealer fool,
Hustler,
Car rustler,
Family buster,
Surge of the hood with his "gofer" crew?

Sound like any dumbass zombies you know?
Suck the life out your bro?
Squeeze money out a ho?
Enough said living dead vampires,

Donnie C's got to
"Thunder Ball"
And
Thunder Roll

Like an avalanche
From a snowcap so high
There's no stopping
The tumble,
The rumble

There's no stemming
The pristine, crystalline tide
Like a tsunami wave
None can ride

Grey Spectre's
Reclaiming lives
Grey Spectre's
Saving souls

Flipping scripts
Changing roles
Cashing chips
Reversing goals

Get in line
Or
Hock your soul
The price is higher
Than today's price of gold

Better be careful
With the company you keep
Grey Spectre's cleaning houses
Dirt devils used to keep

SWINE ON THE MIKE

By Donald T. Williams

Me, Myself, and Eye
Stupid rap motherfucker don't know his name
Said I didn't want "no drama"?
Drama's about to be my claim to fame

Natural born writer
Educated, trained, and tooled
Backbreaking teacher
Will crack you with the ruler

Think you're mean?
My words are cool and crueler
Have you in the dunce's corner
Crying and snotty-nose drooling

Mess with grown folks
Be aware of this
Ain't no grown-ass nigga folks
Gonna take no shit!

Send your boys to ill or kill me
Better come with it quick
Still gonna bleed you like a pig
Put your fat ass on the pit, see if you can still spit

Spic, spit and spite
Are all that I have for you
You started this pig shit,
But it will stop when I'm through

In the meantime,
Twist and tuck your pigtail,
Run, and Bitch, watch where you walk
Find your full-figured fat ass a silhouette in chalk

Me, Myself, and Eye
Stupid rap motherfucker don't know his name
Said I didn't want "no drama"?
Drama's about to be my claim to fame

Mess with grown folks
Be aware of this
Ain't no grown-ass nigga folks
Gonna take no shit!
So you're gangsta?
So you're hard?
Big ham ass, motherfucker
You're a Super-Sized tub of lard

Bragging about how you got me,
How you "snatched my life and my shine"
Spotlights on your fat ass now
Clothed or naked on the spit,
That there derriere
Is a major crime

If there's any question
About whether or not
Two "unknown" lives can collide,
Check your epidermis,
Chicharrones
Best believe
Your pork skin is fried

Really don't give a fuck
Really don't give a shit
Made yourself a target, Porky
And targets do get hit

FYI

By Donald T. Williams

Let's not forget
About Lil Scrappile
Nigger bragged his dick
Was as long as a mile

Twenty-six inches
In between his thighs
Heard that motherfucker
Poked out his own eye

Heard the nigger did it
Trying to Colgate his new grill
Came so hard between his gums
He had a toxic spill

Like you told me
My __'_ Mother fucker
"Don't be offended"
You all day sucker!

And by the way,
Phatback Joe, from the Bronx
How's that Pandemic?
Does it still rain when you want?

Now, don't take it personal
It's just business you know
Like when you took my ___
And made that bitch your whore

You said she was nothing,
But you made her "something"
Didn't you?
Demon boar most cruel

This shit
Is realer than you think
The Mother fucking
Load is you

Don't take it personal
It's just business you know
Don't be offended
Just respect my flow but don't count my dough

Donnie C's here
So the world will know
One cheating, money loving, monkey bitch
Can't stop my show

Hey, Lil Scrappile
Did you buy that yacht?
Spend your days sailing
And tying your dick in knots?

What's your other nasty pastime
While you're on your boat,
Crapping in the ocean
To see if your ship, I mean, shit still floats?

Do yourself a favor
And take your long dick in your hands,
Wrap some long dick around your neck,
And make a long hang noose, man

To the mast or anchor
Knot the rest and off you go,
Swinging long in the wind,
Or long, down to Davey Jones' locker long below

PIMP'S WOE

By Donald T. Williams

Keep pimping
'Til I pop you
Squeeze you
'Tween index and thumb

Blackhead's pus toppings
Ranks for popping
'Til none
I am done

Force yourselves
On innocence
Make them kiss
Your athlete's feet

Make them feel
There's nothing worse
Than the pain
You can unleash

I am the Avenger
And the Answer
Too
All threats

I am the Redeemer
Who
Turns in and out
What evil gets

Was tender mercy given
On the virgin's bloodstained sheets,
Was tender mercy given
When a semened anus secretes?

Woe
No longer the discrete thing
Woe
The horrors it will bring

Sodomize
Blister lips
Words you speak
Sound of a hiss

Rapture's transport
An unarmed embrace
Pimp and viper
One the snake

Agent of the Demon's creed
Orgy's fest on DVD
Evil eyes will sit and watch
As the pimp, they too, will pop

Keep pimping
'Til I pop you
Squeeze you
'Tween index and thumb

Blackhead's pus toppings
Ranks for popping
'Til none
I am done

This you can be certain
Endless will be the hurting
When defiled the child,
Vengeance be worst of wild

Keep pimping
'Til I stop you
Chop you down
Sickle to wheat

Seldom sever mercy
As the Reaper
Never
Sleeps

Pimps up
Ho's down?
Pimps down
Woes up!

Unlock human beings from the sex trade, Money Grip
Hope you can read, Pimp; suck my script!

MOSQUITOES AND GNATS

By Donald T. Williams

Girls,
Women,
Ladies,
And whores

Ain't nothing like them
Why would a "man" ever strike or hurt one?
Donnie C had to write a National Anthem
Calling for a stop to the violence heaped on some

Love the ladies
Yes, I do!
Short ones,
Tall ones,
Are all cool

Petite,
Voluptuous,
Big boned,
Or thick
If she's full female
I can't help but dig

Some are sweet
In the kindest way
Some are treacherous
And will completely dismay

Best not scorn one
'Cause if you do,
Nothing but a world of hurt
In store for you

Girls,
Women,
Ladies,
And whores

Lesser, little, angry "macho" mosquito men
Choose to mistreat
Hell bent on digging bigger holes
In a secreted seat

Girls,
Women,
Ladies,
And whores

Lesser, pesky, angry mosquito men
Like to hit, bite, bleed, and beat
Gotcha on the corner or in the kitchen
If you can stand the heat

If they're not beating,
They're abusing in bed
Tearing tender places
'Til they bleed bloody red

Mixed-up misconceptions
About love, lust, consent, and rape
Ecstasy and roofies
Are the main ingredients of a date rape

Can't and don't complain
If that's your thing,
Some can't come
Without sex's pain, stink, and sting

Give those "alpha blood suckers"
All your juices and goods
Nothing better for a girl in our sexy world
Than a hard piece of thick, trick wood

Who needs a wedding or a ring?

All that gold and diamonds
"Your mouth, pussy, and ass" bought aren't yours,
But "his" bling bling, the scumbag Pimp King

Don't complain
If that's your thing;
Some can't come
Without sex's pain, stink, and sting

Heard a lot of girls, women, ladies, and whores
Have been put through this of late
Something must be wrong
Because this is something I hate

Let these "angry alpha mosquito bastards"
Earn and pay their way
Suck a dick or get fucked themselves
If they want to get paid

Women on the street
Stand tall like golden wheat
Why make the bread
And have some SOB tell you, you can't eat?

Blood sucker tries
To cut you down
Bust some caps
In that clown's crown

Get yourself a few .40s,
But,____ don't get drunk,
Cap that dumb dome with the chrome
And say, "I killed a nasty skunk"

Claim self-defense
With common sense
And have the Judge send you home
Because the jury's convinced

If you need protection,
Then protect yourself;
Cap him in his knees
Ask, "When's the last time you knelt?"

Love the ladies
Yes, I do!
Short ones,
Tall ones,
Are all cool

Petite,
Voluptuous,
Big boned,
Or thick
If she's full female
I can't help but dig

Some are sweet
In the kindest way
Some are treacherous,
And will completely dismay
Best not scorn one
'Cause if you do,
Nothing but a world of hurt
In store for you

"Oh say can you see
The Royalty in me
How dumb can you be
To use and abuse Royalty?

Men can be Kings,
But a Queen also must reign
Let's practice love
And put an end to this pain

Nations rise
Nations fall
There must be
Equality for one and all

Donald T. Williams

Good for the gander
Good for the goose
Anything less
Good to cut you loose

Step on me
I will "nine inch steel heel" stomp back!
Put some hard, impervious wood
Down your throat and up your crack!

Maybe you'll "like it"
Maybe you won't
As long as you "come" to understand
That "No" means "Don't"!

Oh, say can you see
The Royalty in me
How dumb can you be
To use and abuse Royalty?

Bring back slavery
As a sexual thing,
The Death Knell
For you,
Shall surely ring"

Grey Spectre
And
Donnie C
Take a stand and command

Castration
Of more "sick" dicks
Euthanasia
Is the answer
For these sick dogs and their tricks

Without a working tool,
These emasculated
Or
Dead head fools
Can wet dream

And
"Imaginate"
A hand free masturbate
With an invisible prick

Think that's sick?
Got a bone to pick?
Grey Spectre
And
Donnie C
Out to make
Pimps pay like tricks

Halloween will come daily
Even sooner for some
Grey Spectre's a vengeful ghost,
And you don't want none

There's a Revolution coming,
Summoning
True Independence Proclamations
Freedom,
Newly embraced again

Sex slaves will be freed
All sexual slavery will end
All those who oppose
Contact your next of kin

Sex slaves will be freed
All sexual slavery will end
All those who oppose
Burn in the fiery wind

Such winds are selective
Instinctively,
Know where to turn
Fiery winds are intelligent
God has taught well;
They have learned

Winds of fire are patient

Fiery winds await the Command
Once the "go ahead" is given
Fiery headwinds will scorch the land

No points on the compass
Point to the "saving grace place"
Such winds are selective,
But posthaste is their pace

Free the sex slaves
Nat Turner style
Old Nat Turner's "go ahead"
Makes Grey Spectre smile

They'll try to beat you,
Whip you,
Shoot you,
Dog maul you,
Lynch you
Without a trial

Learn how to fight and shoot, Lady Killer
Bust them up close
Or
Pick them off at half a mile

Free the sex slaves
Nat Turner style
What
Donnie C
And
The Grey Spectre
Say
Makes Old Nat Turner smile

GO TO SLEEP MAGGIE
By Donald T. Williams

There's a bitch named Maggie
I've come to berate
Bullshit _____-_-__
And a nigger "first rate"

Sent by evil____
To see me in jail
Why'd the bum bitch come
If she came without bail?

Listened to my storied plight,
Made me think I'd be alright,
Left the joint with my keys and ID,
Didn't come back, and cracked "The fuck with bailing me."

That's some really low down
Nigger "family" shit
Niggers call her "Bullet"
And I wish she'd get hit

Pissing on her grave
Is what I plan "to do" for you
Piss on ____ first,
Then piss on bum bitch, "Bullet" when I'm through

Mind you, I've known these "family" niggers
For more than thirty years
Always showed them love
And nothing but good cheer

When the chips were down,
Everyone turned their back
All that "family" love
Was just a bullshit act

Knowing their true nature
Breeds disgust in me
Only their dead faces
Is what I long to see

I know
What you're thinking
It's ungodly
To wish anyone the grave,
But you don't know
These zombies
How deceptively
They behave!

Always laughing and jiving
These jigaboos will make a nigga feel at home
Always cooking and eating
There's plenty of fried fish, corn bread, collard greens, and neck
bones

A minion like you, Maggie
Can come and go from Hell
Telltale signs are unforgiving
Counterfeit Chanel
Can't hide your hog farm smell

There's a bum bitch named Maggie
I've come to berate
Bullshit _____-_-__
And a nigger "first rate"

"Family" niggers call her "Bullet"
How I wish that she'd get __!
Made herself a target
And I really don't give a shit

Toad in a skirt needs croaking,
Frog legs fried to a crisp
Butt burning grease
Is but a pond
Won't hurt her black ass one bit

When you get back to Hades, Maggie
Say hello to Ma for me
You know, I kind of miss her
Strange as that can be

Made yourself a target, Maggie
Hard target,
Colder than a witch's tit
Laser paints your pickle nipple, Maggie
How I wish that you'd get__!

WHAT'S UP WITH THAT?

By Donald T. Williams

Some niggers are low
To the highest degree
Such would be the case
For this nigger, Easy E

This cutthroat motherfucking _____
Must come under attack
Love and loyalty
Is what this nigger lacks

Wouldn't come and get me
When I was locked up in jail
Bullshit gun charges on me,
And he don't come with my bail

Niggers locked in Guiltyford County, NC
Keep the CO's in jobs
Crooked cops and robbers
With strong ties to the mob's knob

23 and 1
Is how they had me locked up in jail
Buck fifty
Is all I needed to make bail

Easy E just got a new car
But moves like a snail
Suppose to be my _____
But he don't act like he's male

He don't hear my call
No matter how I shout
All I have is up for grabs
If I don't get out

Slimy motherfucker
Did me grimy like that
Nigger is my _____
But he's more like a rat

Couldn't be that "A" Town
Is so far away
Nigger could have bailed me
And been home the same day

What's up with that my _____,
Someone in your ass too deep,
Years gone by and from you
I haven't heard a squeak?

That's okay my _____
Maybe you can't talk
That's okay my _____
Maybe you can't walk

Creeps you've laid down with
Made the bed where you sleep
Don't feel sorry for you, nigger
Not one tear will I weep

Do feel sorry for my ___ _____,
Sweet Cymone
Hurt when you told me
Don't call her on the phone

Guess she's old enough
To start working the ___
I bet you would ___ your own _____, the precious pearl;
I bet Daddy would make it rain for his big, little girl

If that's the way
You say it has to be, Pimp Daddy
She still has my love,
And that will always be

To add insult to injury, I haven't heard
From two grown ass ___

Guess they must be angry?
Think their _____'_ a bum?

It can't be
Either one of these_____
Came from my nut sack and cum!
I may have played Daddy,
But I am bio ____ to none

Dirty, ___ of a witch
Mama's ___ are no excuse
Gutless traitors of Donnie C
Are of no _____ use

What's up with that?
Drop a nigger ice cold?
Must be more to this story
Than what I've told

You niggers got secrets
Too dark to unload
You can hold the waters back
As long as the dam holds

But things of man
Aren't built to last
God will help you with your burden,
But you must yield, kneel, and be humble to ask

If you're too caught up in the world,
And don't know like I know
Get that burden off your chest, niggas
Breathe!
Let it go

If not, niggers
Hold that gas
Don't let it pass
No one can tell you
What to do with that ass

If not, niggers
Hold in
The dark you know
With family members like you
A nigga like me
Is better off
In the light
Alone

Don't have much else
To say to you
I've pretty much sold out the store,
But another shipment is due

What comes around goes around
Like a spinning top on the floor
So, it won't be long before I restock
And diss you niggas some more

ON THE HOOK

By Donald T. Williams

Be informed and listen up
Listen up please

I know others have been involved
In dastardly deeds concerning Donnie C

Donnie C can't let you off the hook
Because in an act of malice you partook

Marie Jane Blight, I heard you mention my ex-___ '_ and my name
At the end of one of your songs

The song was very good
And you really didn't say anything that wrong

So Marie Jane, you can be at ease
I like your work and your singing does please

But, Bedon'tsay, I should bring you to your ashy knees
Hope that's rug burn, or has CraZy, that nigga, given you a disease?

Did he put his magnum .44
To your head,
On your rack,
In your snatch,
Far up your crack?

What do you see in him?
God only knows
Girls will be girls
Ho's will be ho's

From "this asshole"
Chocolate cookie "dough" goes

You know your taste
You know your brown nose

You
Seem like a nice girl
You
Don't appear to be just some whore
He'd strap down for his "around the world" tour

Nonetheless, Donnie C. hopes
You had a lovely wedding day

Did you read your new husband a children's book?
Give him some Play Doh and let him honeymoon play?

Hope CraZy, that nigga, can resist your pretty face and the crack in
your back
Get around to the front

Make you two a baby
Not just serve your pretty head his blistered blunt

Happier days for you may be ahead
Give it time

The going will be "slow" with him
But if it's love, you won't mind

"Let's not judge a book by its cover" is the best
People are known to say

Keep CraZy, that nigga, away from all those kitchen chemicals and
garden weeds
And please, please read to him every day

Let's see who else
Donnie C's got on his list?

Who else done gone
And got Donnie C pissed?

Some Fudgee motherfucker,
I think Ycleflip is his name

Sang a song on one of Marie Jane Blight joints
About Donnie C's hurt and pain

Hatin' nigga got it right when he said
That bitch shot me down

I may have hit the dirt hard,
But she didn't put Donnie C in the ground

911
Should have been my speed dial call,

But I don't trust the cops;
They've never helped me at all

If you know you're dirty
And Donnie C left you out some way,

The nigger was in remiss,
But don't gloat; be thankful you got away

Donnie C's not in the habit
Of handed out mean spirited disses,

But Donnie C just had to school you niggers
Now you are dissed and dismissed

I'm a BEAST!
Verbal nightmare to say the least

I'm a BEAST!
Blowing up fast like bread with yeast

I'm a BEAST!
Donnie C's fame and glory in the cards stacked to increase

I'm a BEAST!

Royal Flush,
Crappy, rapper motherfuckers!
Read them,
Wipe your ass with the cards, tards
And
Weep

Don't feel sorry for you
Really don't give a shit

Made yourself a target
And targets do get hit

PROBLEM REVOLVER

By Donald T. Williams

I'm the problem
That won't go away
I'm the problem
That's here to stay

I'm the problem
That can't be solved
I'm the problem
On which your every thought revolves

All the time you suckers spent
Trying to make a fool of me
All of your distain
All of your mockery

Turns out to be your own shit
Messing up your fine sneakers and shoes
Turns out to be your own excrement
Stinking and sticking like CraZy glue

Ain't it funny, Phatback Joe
How, as this world turns
There are several lessons
"Rich but hungry" assholes like you can learn?

First, Barbecued, Babyback, Bronx Bomber,
Better learn to leave every day, hardworking people alone
You can't steal what's theirs,
Try to make it your own

Second, Lil Scrappile with the mile long dick
Honest hustlers like me always get back their shit
Stop "sucking yours" and brushing your 45 thou' teeth
That's some smile, but damn, good grief!

77,000 x 77,000 x 77,000 . . .
Equals a fair amount
You hip hop niggers love money so much
So, I guess you niggers can count

All except for Two Quarters
Fifty cent is a high as he goes
Nigga said, "Don't ask me who's the last one who rammed her"
"Petite Change" claimed he didn't know
Well, I'm asking anyway, Bullet Proof
And, in the simplest addition,
I'm also asking too,
If you signed Lil Scrappile for 100 mil,
What was my Khris due?

Bred to live
Born to die
Did you niggers
Make my ___ cry?

All your muscles,
Bumped up dicks
Had my ___
Turning tricks?

Ate Balls,
Mouthful bragging 'bout flipping bricks
That beautiful "brick house" is "forever" mine, glutton
Believe that shit!

"Popped Khristal
Like you pop a beer?"
_____ boys to "down low" men
"Does" make you queer, you hear!

Alpha Hog,
Pork barrel bitch!
Do anything to make your black ass rich?
Well, dig this:

187

Donald T. Williams

There's a cue stick in Hell,
Ate Balls
Chalked and waiting for you
Rack after rack
Giving "your" phat, black crack"
Its eternal due

It's you
Alpha Hog,
Dog,
Motherfatherchildfuckers
Donnie C
Really can't stand

Think
I'll rid the world of you,
Degenerates
Think
Mass extinction,
Like the dinosaur, Can Can man

Don't think it can happen?
Ever heard of bitch slapping?
Don't shut your eyes!
Don't blink!

Find your asses in Hades
_____ your asses
Watching them "wink"
Smelling their eternal stink

Sounds like what you're used to,
How bad can it be?
Fool niggers said, "Lord, please "don't" have mercy;
Sounds like "another" party!"

Freaks of nature
With the Cruel AIDS smiles
As you ejaculate
In or on a child

Smile now
You shameless clowns
In a sea of your own semen
You will surely drown

An endless torture,
An endless swim
For you,
Will soon begin

Swim to sink
Sink to swim
Like victims of an uncapped well
With too much oil to skim

Is there a hint
Of forgiveness
In your fate?

Is there a slim chance
You may squeeze
By slippery sleaze
Through the Narrow Gate?

Can't tell
What God foresees
Guess you'll have to enema,
Sit,
Shit,
And
Wait

Even fools like you
Can figure out
77,000 x 77,000 x 77,000 . . .
Is a pretty fair count,
An obscene amount

Of demons
Pulling your trigger,
Bouncing your ass,
Making your sack quiver

That's a long, long time
Spent on your knees
Taking it and screaming
Like a helpless child begging, "Please!"

Are you an ass loving
__ _____ social disease?
Are you "a fuck age and gender"
Social travesty?

Motherfatherchildanimalfucking
Son of a bitch!
Was your father a warlock?
Was your mother a witch?

Pimp,
Hustler,
Rapper,
Dealer
Pedophile,
Alpho, Alpha, John Doe Money Grip
Donnie C's here
And he's a Grand Canyon trip

I'm the problem
That won't go away
I'm the problem
That's here to stay

Don't give a fuck
If you're hard,
On the down low,
Or
Straight out gay
With my family
And
Dough
You suckers should have never played

So,
Come at me,
But
Atheists,
Agnostics
Know this:
I'm rolling in righteous thunder;
Him,
Who's keeping me,
You can't hit

Shameless clowns
Say you don't believe
Come at me
This
Whole Wide World
Will Grieve

I'm the problem
That won't go away
I'm the problem
That's here to stay

I'm the problem
That can't be solved
I'm the problem
On which every thought

Revolves

Donald T. Williams

YEAH, YOU HEARD RIGHT

By Donald T. Williams

Yeah, you heard right, motherfucker
I'm off the hook
Snatching up
Every damn thing you took

That's right, motherfucker
I'm off the chain
Don't try to get with me;
You'll try in vain

Donnie C's here;
Things won't be the same
Out to set the record straight
And make a name

Out to break all records
Bring you suckers
To suckle
On the sour nipple of shame

Big bad, nigga names
In the game
Need Donnie C's chainsaw
To cut against your grains

Yes, your paper
Came from countless trees,
But Grey Spectre will chop you down
To a Timberlame stump,
Toad stool,
Below the knees

CraZy, that nigga and his Fuck a Fella,
Justa Timberswamp,

Lil Scrappile,
Petite Change, and Phatback Joe

Some of these SOB's
I'm sure you know
Donnie C's new on the scene,
And his work you know but don't know

These Titanics,
Laden hulls,
Filled with platinum, diamonds, and gold,
Have pirated, bitten, and ripped off
Donnie C's or his___'_ genius and flow

While in a crack fog so thick,
How could the grand slamming
Base head know?
When his "not knowing"
Was their goal

Now it's Donnie C's time
To set sail and flow to places unknown,
Rise and shine
Like the Sun,
Phoenix or a paragon diamond
Let his brilliance show

So, you can keep the ____
She's old, damaged goods
Plenty more fine ladies
In our nation's hoods

Matter of fact,
President Obama's First Lady
Is very much my ideal
Integrity,
Brains,
Beauty,
Class,
Compassion,
Style,

And
So much,
So much
Sex appeal

But don't worry
My brother,
My earthy,
Commander and Chief

I'd never want what's yours
I'm waiting for my soul mate,
Perhaps that old ____,
To walk through my door
I'm not like some ___ stealing
___ raping male whores
Sweating steroids
Out their pores

___ fucking motherfuckers
With pumped up dicks they boast
Stuffing one between their boys' cheeks
When they want a
One,
Two,
Or
Three Way
Down low
Romper room,
Hide and Seek the Salami,
Beefy rump roast

Alpha males
Or
So they hail
Seems too freaky,
Caligula,
Dead civilization,
Strange to me

I'm Donnie C,
I'm what you see
What a true "Man"
Worth
His
Earth
Dirt
Clay
Sand
Or
Salt
Should be!

PART FIVE
SEX IN THE SOUTHERN CITY

BBS HOOKERS
RR aka WFFD
DISHONORABLE JMGX
XXX THREAT—TRIPLE THREAT
BUSTED BACK DOOR
TO THE WHITE MAN
SHITTY GRITS
SOMETHING NASTY
KNOW DOUBT?
IT'S ENOUGH
C U D

BBS HOOKERS

By Donald T. Williams

Absolute Blister,
A little smut shop I know
In the town of Lombertin, NC
Where I used to go

Stopped in, looked around
But then, the clerk gave me
One particular DVD
She suggested I see

BBackk Street Hookers I believe;
No. I'm sure that was the name
I looked at front cover, did a double take,
And stared at it again

What grabbed my mind's attention:
The bitch's "Good Gracious Jones!"
Back bumper's position
Dropped hot on the cover's front
Shit looked just like my ___'_ dumper
As many times as I ____ her
And I wondered, "Aw Shucks!
What the fuck?"

More than just confused
I was dismayed and completely shocked
Photo on the back
Had her "far more than familiar" face sucking a cock

Something in her eyes
Gave the whole anguishing shit away
I'd know my baby's eyes
Anywhere,
Any day

Took it home and watched
As the freak show took its course
Hurt beyond all human belief
All I could think of was _____

Deadly curiousness
Nearly killed this inquisitive cat
Cause of the near death experience:
A broken heart attack
Man eater fangs
Had gone for my jugular
Tiger paws
Had swiped at my balls

Grey Spectre
Reappeared
In an instant
Is all I gladly
Recall

Supernatural reflexes
Went into full effect
Eyes had seen the truth
But with such anguish, such regret

Then on top of that
Here comes another "recognizable" nigger I know
Wise cracking Black Judge on the
JMGX TV show

Nigger had been at FayFartville State
A month or so ago
Now, here's this nigger in a XXX
Busting out some young ass ho

Now I know for a fact
My ___ was always watching his show
He comes to town to give a speech,
And here they are in the same freak show

Coincidences like these
Are far and few in between
Shit I could live without
If you know what I mean

That's when everything for me
Started to go pretty bad
The shit had hit the fan
And almost drove me mad

There's more to this story
You can surely believe me
Donnie C's a straight shooter,
And I know what I have seen

Anybody got a copy
Of the DVD I spoke about?
Left mine around for stealing
It was stolen
So I have no doubts

Funny thing about these motherfuckers
Is their pleasure in being cruel
Left me a DVD like it
Without the Judge,
That cunt eating fool

This one had the title
BBlackk Street Hookers produced by Tee Tee
Just as gross and graphic
As the original,
BBackk Street Hookers DVD

By the way,
Here's some more you should know
As much as it hurts,
I still love her so

Don't feel sorry for you
Really don't give a shit
Made yourself a target
And targets do get hit

RR aka WFFD

By Donald T. Williams

Roxxxy Raynalds
Is her aka name
Porn Queen Diva
Of the sex trade game

WFFD is what
I knew her by
A lovely ___
But man, this bitch was sly

Roper doped and sucker punched me
With a deadly blow
Never thought this ___ of mine
Could be a low down whore

But, seeing is believing or deceiving
And I got the full view
What she did was pretty ugly
God have mercy on you

God,
Please have mercy
Because Satan's got her soul
Hope and pray
We don't burn apart or together
In his pit below

God,
Please hear my prayers
And let our souls be saved
Try to make amends
Before we're in our graves

Donald T. Williams

The Spirit Made Me Do It
The Devil Made Me Do It Too
Hope
Dear God is merciful
On we two

DISHONORABLE JMGX

By Donald T. Williams

Honorable JMGX
Is how he likes to be known

TV Judge
On a self-righteous throne

From the hood,
Through the trenches,
And now
On the bench

Only problem is
Donnie C
Smells his stench

Caught him in a XXX
Without his black robe
Eating jailbait fish
Had the little hoochie pumping him
As he wiggled his toes

"Here comes the Judge!"
Now,
Who can fault him for that?
A wife or girlfriend,
Perhaps,
May smell a black rat?
Most brothers like tartar sauce
With some extra,
Et cetera,
Hot sauced trim
Especially,
When the whore
Is fine, thick, and younger than him

What I didn't like
Was this nigger's wise cracks
About crack heads and their crack
If a nigga lights the fuse,
Has a blast like that,
What's this nigger got to say
When I've seen his ass crack?

Some of you have seen
This DVD I've seen too!
Know damn well
How the hell
"This nigger do"

Caught this
Dishonorable, Nigger Judge wrong and strong
Tongue
Lickety-split
Lick lapping left side of a thong,
But
This Black,
"Unrobed"
Nigger's going to act like he's better than you

Let me hold up here
Before I further digress
Hate the day I ever
Got caught up in this mess

Donnie C
Simply wants to clear the air
Can't stand to see a hypocrite
Arrogantly, seated in a high chair
A bitch on her knees
Under his robe
Her thumb in his ass
Knuckle deep in the probe

Looking down,
Cracking wise,
False,
Fishy face nigger
I despise

Nigger's waste deep
In body fluids,
In his own slime
He and pig,
Twins of swine

Dishonorable JMGX
Is how he should be known
Hypocritical nigger,
Better leave us crack heads alone

XXX THREAT—TRIPLE THREAT

By Donald T. Williams

Once I caught
Your nasty ass
I got in the wind
And I got there fast

Just how long
You did me wrong?
Don't care much now
Just glad I'm gone

Never thought
That I would see
My June ____
Make a fool of me

Daisy Mae's taken off
In a strip tease flick
Thong pulled aside
Reveals vivacious vulva lips

Lips and an ass
I thought were mine
My sweet country girl
Committing marital crime

Wouldn't hurt as bad
If she just had an affair
Bitch had to show the whole world
How much she didn't care

Blindside a loving _____
Was it pure hate?
Mindless rage
Is up for debate

A scorned woman's revenge
Will make any man cringe
I'm willing to confess
I've cheated now and then,

But nothing I could have done
Deserved betrayal like this
Satan, the wicked snake
Wooed her with his hiss

Defiled her every hole
With a twenty-six inch dick
Mind and body snatched
For turning tricks

Never heard my baby
Scream for me like that
Wailing like a child
With a torch up her crack

These are not the stuff
Sweet dreams are made of
Nightmarish screams
Of the woman I loved

Played out
On a XXX DVD
Marketed
For the freakish world
To see
But
Made
Especially,
To hurt me

Granted, motherfuckers
You had a big time pay day
I would waste you all
If I could have my way

For
Like rats and roaches
Love the dark to hide
You're in the shadows,
Munching on the cheese
Made off that smut worldwide

Donnie C's floodlight
Is shining on your dirty crew
Donnie C's the man who's going to chew, spit, dispose,
And expose you

Go on and start
Squealing like the pigs you are
Donnie C's got you pickled
And you're in his jar

BUSTED BACK DOOR

By Donald T. Williams

Phatback Joe burped he had a German Unit
___ ___ my ___
Said there was no fixing her
That she'd be ___ _____ for life

Lil Scrappile said "You ain't getting love
If it ain't from the "A"
These assholes' words
Have haunted me to this very day

XXX DVD confirmed for me
That it was true
Damage had been done
There wasn't anything I could do

Well Phatback, Two Tons of Pork,
Bronx Bomber, Swine on the Mike
Donnie C's ranting on you
I know you hear all the hype

Sticks and stones can break my bones
But not like the pain I must bear
That Deuce Four had belonged to me,
But you didn't care

Now she's just a dollar bill
A buck fifty and no more
Donnie C's never a victim
Donnie C settles the score

Shoot me dead and kill me
I'm Hell bound or to Heaven sent
Either way, I was only potter's dust
Or gun smoke from the cartridges I spent

Donnie C's not going to ride you
Like that sadistic German Unit rode that poor, misguided ___ and
___

Bounce you like a beach ball
Busting Bronco's back door

Donnie C's going to say his piece
And settle all the scores
Donnie C's going to make a mint
A hundred Goldfingers would adore

Don't feel sorry for you
Really don't give a shit
Made yourself a target
And targets do get hit

Bull's eye
Like an asshole
Donnie C's bullets
Fly straight or curve

Either way,
Donnie C hits you
Tearing flesh,
Breaking bones,
And
Severing nerves

Don't feel sorry for you
Really don't give a shit
Made yourself a target
And targets do get hit

TO THE WHITE MAN

By Donald T. Williams

To the White man
Who defiled my ambitious ___
May you spend an eternity in Hell
Endure an endless plunge
Of the fleshy knife

Because
You told her
To kiss you
To scream, "Please!", "More!"
To me
She was an honorable _____
To you
A whore to explore, notch, and score

Despite
The pain in her eyes
Despite
The strain in her veins
Black Mare, the trophy
Black Mail, the game
Black Maria, the Patrol Wagon
Black Man, the bigger game
Black Panther, the armed militant
Black Power, the village armed, educated, and trained

Disbelief
In God,
Disregard
For wedded life,
May your families,
Friends,
And
My foes
Experience

Donald T. Williams

Exactly what it's like

To have
One's honor trampled,
To have
One's name disgraced,
To hear
The screams of tortured ecstasy,

To see
The freakish,
Contorted face
Of a ___
Reduced to chattel
In an underworld sewer tanning shop
For rawhide

Sordid scum
Pumps
Through the hearts of the wicked
In their sodomy
Is their pitiless pride

Who
Will bring to slaughter
The "animals"
Responsible
For this?

My Father
Wields
The ultimate death blow
With a mere flick if His wrist

Did not
Sodden and Gomorra
One doomsday
Cease to exist?
Did not
My Father's writings entreat you
Do you still not get the gist?

Spelled out
All the simpler
Like getting one's ducks in a row
You shall reap what you sow

Just as in time,
The mourning rooster did crow
Just as the Savior foretold it to be so;
The coward who loved Him
Did let his true nature show
Says the "Duke of Ducks"
You thought a "pigeon"
Pray this man has Christ
More than just religion
To the White man
Who defiled my ambitious ___
May you spend an eternity in Hell
Endure an endless plunge of the long knife

Because
You told her to kiss you,
To scream,
"Please!" "More!"
To me
She was a treasure, _____, ___
To you
She was a whore
To bore and notch as an ass scored

Despite
The pain in her eyes
Despite
The strain in her veins
Black Mare, the trophy
Black Mail, the game
Bet you're a cop!
Bet you're a pig!
Officer Donatello Williamson,
With a Fayfartville, NC Law Enforcement gig

Escort to my last dance

Donald T. Williams

Six inch needle to my thigh
Rueful involuntary commitment
"Oh so obvious" the lie!
Black Maria, the Patrol Wagon
Black Man, the bigger game
Black Panther, the armed militant
Black Power, the community armed, educated, and trained

Conspiracy
Set in motion,
Am I to die tonight?
Miraculous
My recovery
Next day, my eyes shine bright
What be this commotion,
As if they've seen a ghost?
Eyes tinged red with frutescence
Frankincense,
My Holy,
Oil dipped burnt toast!
Phatback Joe,
The candy wrapper,
Spitted gum
Stuck on my shoe,
Or
Is that stick
Feces,
Excrement
Laid by the whore or you?

Really doesn't matter
I'll make something out of nothing too
Stick it
On my laptop turntable,
Scratch it
Like a platter
Boom platinum tunes
For fans to consume
Watch my overweight
As my deep pockets get phatter

You've already claimed
Enough drama and shame,
But
You've failed to autograph it
You
Neither know nor know
How to sign your name,
Yet,
Somewhere
There's a taboo tattoo
Someplace
On my ex-boo
Indelible ink "Can" be erased
Even the Devil's mark
And the foul odor of you

Stamped with his approval
My God can countermand its removal
Yes,
That lost soul is not yours to keep
I,
As _____,
Shall reclaim her
And this,
If anything,
You can believe,
XXX
Will be the Devil's payment
In pain and suffering,
As my God's prices
Are most grave,
Most steep
For demons of the deep

Verses rapped from the Lil Scrappile
Rise and fill the air
Filth has now gone airborne
Permeates the clean, fresh air
Poison takes its new form
The toxic songs of me

Soon as I inhale it
Monsters let go,
Give rise to me,
My victory

How Tricky Three Triple Crosses!
Are they X's,
Are they T's?
My Father's
Boss of Bosses
Doctor of Love;
Doctor of Misery!
I dare say,
Dr. Feelgood?
Will be
The opposite you get?
Black man
In the cracked mirror
Lollipop sucker
Caught in the net?

Anglers use many methods
To capture the Big Fish
Unhook the sturdy hook
From its mouth
Chop off the head
Or serve the entire body on a dish
Sportsmen with their arsenal
Use many methods too
To capture the Big Fish
For food or fun is what they do

Pull on lines for seconds,
Minutes, hours, or days
Struggle
Does the Big Fish
Against
The old man of the sea
As he fights
To break away,
To break free,
To break the line

Of the strongest test
Has no interest in who is best,
Knows the seas
The Father has blessed
Succumbs
To the hook
Concedes
The need
To rest

Will the Big Fish
Face the dinner plate,
Will the Big Fish
Endure the mutilate,
Will fresh fish fins
Be brutally removed,
Will my loving Father
Furiously disapprove?

Verses
Rapped by Lil Scrappile
Rise and fill
The air
Filth
Has now gone airborne
What's done can't be undone;
Nonetheless,
Where's my __'_ share?

Even I,
As proud ____,
Can't help but gravitate to the landfill
To the verbal stench
That makes as much sense
As my __'_ beats
Rising from the mound
As skillful, artistic, melodic sound
Millions
Of the ocean's dead fish
Rotting and festering
Become the now

Land bound
A blackhead rising,
Raising pain
The swollen, swelling mound smells of rot
The steamy Yellow Stone park grounds
One fine doomsday will hurl,
"Will" self destruct, "will" pop

Like a King of Pop Music
Like a culture popped
Like a bag of Orville Redneckracker's Colonels
Microwaved,
Bold and brave,
Buttered butt steamy hot,
And primed for shots
Don't ask. Don't tell.
Why the fuck not?

Lil Scrappile's landfill
"Can't" be a graveyard
Not if my __ shares a spot
Bodies like garbage,
Ton on Ton on Top
"Hm?
Ton on Ton on Top . . .
Look!
There goes a Triple T;
Good God,
I'd better stop!"

That may be a super nova
"No! No!"
But I'm sure you failed to check
Treat women
Like a "Yo, yo, ho!"
Spinning tricks with a bitch's collar and leash around her neck
Will be your last trick I bet
Halloween comes early,
Yet right on time, as my Lord, Jesus divine
Those who love the pagan can party,
But for the last time

Trick or Treat
As Pirates
Trick or Treat
As Pigs
Trick of Treat
As PD's, CO's, Lawyers, or Judges
Like those who robbed
My guns, cars, truck, and freshly decked out crib

Now,
Comes home the soldier,
PTSD
Whacked out from Triple Traumatizing Tours
In Afghanistan
After four of a kind
In Iraq
Straight
To local Law Enforcement
Imagine that!
Pray to God Almighty
The "lethal weapon" knows how to act!

Take a tip
From MMMG
You know,
The Ball of Thunder
From Down Under
Flashbacks not a problem
When you live them every day
As is the acquired taste and smell
Of premium, gourmet, "humane", decay
Iraq and Afghanistan,
The scapegoat training grounds,
For what will unfold and further dismay
In ways that will profoundly astound

Homeland Occupation,
Eminent Domain,
Curfews,
And then Martial Law
Enforced by the Dogs of War

Donald T. Williams

Trained in wrestle mania
And my God,
You know they love it "raw"
In the cage of rage Octagon fights
Where biting off a nose or ear
Is considered a "lover's" bite
Untrained,
Empty handed
The big civilian,
"People of color",
Flaw
Especially,
The valiant Black man
Aside and besides
His libido's famous and shameless penis,
His hardened head or steel jaw

Now,
There comes his "soft" behind
The White man's depraved ways
Do and will
Take hold
If given acceptance and time

Brothers need a Hammer, Keith David, Jim Brown, Ving Rhames,
Danny Glover,
Morgan Freeman,
Denzel Washington, Ice Cube, and a Samuel L. Jackson
Who will do more than act

Sisters need a brother man, husband, fiancé, or love
Who knows how to act,
Who rocks steady in the sack,
Pays all the bills
Or
Is qualified to pick up the slack,
Who is present in the home
And always has her back
Well mannered,
Schooled, tooled,
Trained, sober, not cruel,
Considerate, loving, cool,

And nobody's,
Not even her fool

Children need every day,
Positive role models
As well as Legends of cinema and song

Teens need a loving,
Working Father and Mother
Whose support and understanding
Are strong

Babies need a King, Powell, Marshall, Evers, Sharpton, Rangel,
And Obama; they can aspire too!
None of us are perfect
But
Perfect what you can do

Families need a Men and Women
100 Billion Dollar March
To get what's owed and undoubtedly
DUE
None of us are perfect
But
Perfect what you do

Exclude
The "angry" White man though
His trenches
Long ago
Dug so deep
All
The latest weapons
The "White" gunsmiths love to own, shoot,
And lawfully keep
Buy them by the ton
Much cheaper
Is the cost
Warehouse
The ammunition and fuel
Preserve

The frozen or smoked meat and fish
Long since bought

All
Things with long shelf life
Line the storehouse walls
Medicine for cuts and scrapes preempted
For the unseen trip and fall

Chances are their wounded
Will need a doctors' or nurses' care
Surely, in the "White" family,
I'm certain one, if not two dozen, will be there

Call it crucial forethought
A stitch in time saves nine
Inside information,
Like inside trading
For the "White" man and family
Is not a crime
The "wise man" will wonder;
Will take a moment's ponder:
Release and throw it back,
Like a wise angler with some tact

TT,
The fine actor
Tee Tee,
The producers of "Butt Smut"
TT,
The Black man in the mirror
CM,
The lollipop sucker who ran out of luck
Righteousness diminishes
As we worship Silver Screen images
Black Magic Cinema
Turns crap to gold
Miners mine minors,
Tight, tiny, tunnels dug
For feces,
Hit the mother
Of mother lodes

Pirates of land
Pirates of seas
The booty
Is the gain
The booty
Is the same

Smugglers
All around US
Too slick to pay a toll
Too crafty for a census poll
Out to chop off "your" head or hand
Release your grip on ill-gotten cash and gold

Topsy turvey turn tables
Scratch wax,
Synthesize beats
Computers mix and remix
The remix
Triple X the six
Play backwards
The CD disk

Nothing's
Too straight forward
As the CD's and DVD's
Spin around and around
Laser lights point the assassin's shot
Laser lights change electricity's light to sound

Visible images in one's eyes
Audible images in one's ears
Why this Devilish indoctrination?
What motive,
What game,
What gain?

The "wise man"
Will wonder;
The "wise woman"
Will take a moment's ponder:

Release
Throw
It back,
Like a wise angler
With some tact?

A
Few
Wise
Fishermen
Are out there;
Fishers of Men,
I've heard them say
Who's
That tugging on your line,
Or
Does it work the other way?
Who
Pulls on lines for centuries?
Who
Drops nets every night and every day?
Who
Bids you not break the line of strong test
Who
Seeks you
Until His,
The Lord's Day?

Obvious
The answer
Given in the question
One need not ask

Obviously,
He seeks you;
Are you up to the strong test,
The tackle,
The task?

Given the solution,
You need not care the day

All that He has asked you
Is to love Him,
Each other,
And
Obey

To the White man
Who defiled my ambitious ___
May you spend an eternity in Hell
Endure an endless plunge of the long knife

Confess,
Repent,
Take my advice
I ask this once
I won't ask twice

Tossed that ass
Take a ___
Tossed that ass
Take a family,
Take a life
Tossed a salad
Sliced and diced
Sea chowder children
Of your bloodline
Served cold on a bed
Of rancid caviar, maggots, and lice

Much Ado about Everything,
Crazy nigger on crack,
Mid Summer Night's Scream
Then,
Do ignore the fact
Don't act
Don't react
Don't face the opinion's facts,
Or the unwise weisenheimer cracks

Forget
The sound advice
Forget
The "token" smoking peace pipe

Forget
The reasonable plea
Forget
The tender mercies
Forget
The personal responsibility
Forget
The aforementioned fee

Forget
The gratuity,
But
Don't forget
"My" favorite recipe

Bon appétit, Pig!
Can you dig like a pig, Pig?
Lights,
Action,
Camera
That's a take
Or
Was it digitally remastered?
You bastards!

In that case
It's a fake,
But
Not the case
Of my Triple A
Triple X
Berate

What say you,
Poop Dog
Got any mercy

For these hogs,
Yourself,
Iced Cube T,
Phatback Joe,
Lil Scrappile, the "A" he be,
Ate 88 Black Balls x 3,
Or
CraZy, that nigga,
His bitch Bee,
Or
Tee Tee?

Any mercy for a ___
Reduced to chattel
In an underworld,
Sewer tanning shop
For "raw" rawhide?

Sordid scum
Pumps
Through the hearts of the wicked
In their sodomy
Is their pitiless pride

Who
Will bring to slaughter
The "animals"
Responsible
For this?

My Father
Wields the ultimate
Life
Or
Death
Blow
With a simple flick
Of His wrist

As quick
As this

The end
Of your bliss

Sure as
A traitor's kiss,
Thirty pieces of silver
In his back stabbing fist
Soon,
My Father
Will send
The Son

To fulfill
A prophecy,

To grant
A prayer,

To blow
A candle's wish

My Father
Will unclench my fist,
Avenge
For me
The barbarians' diss,

Burn
This sinful world
To a blackened,
Ashy crisp

From the ashes
Comes
The New Birth
Paradise
Is
Heaven on Earth

SHITTY GRITS

By Donald T. Williams

I heard somewhere that freaky people
Are now sprinkling sugar on shit
Mixing it like liver pudding
In a bowl of hominy grits

Pissing and crapping on each other
And calling that "sex"
What in this freaking world
Are you freaky people going to do next?

What will you anal obsessed scum seekers
Standardize next to cast a wider net?
Have you taken into account what eating shitty grits
Can do to your breath?

All you __ fuckers can go your own way
Donnie C don't give a fuck if you're an Alpha Dog,
Low down on the down low
Or straight out gay

Just don't ever mistake me
For being down with that shit
There's something I find unsanitary
About shit on the tip of my noble dick

Ass to mouth
Has never been very "sexy" to me
Never cared for it all the way live
Or in a XXX DVD

If you're a girl or boy
And that brings you joy
If that turns you on,
There's a horse in the barn

229

Donald T. Williams

Mount up and please ride
Until you and horse drop
In a Three-peat Throw Down Triple Crown
That runs for hours nonstop

You're all winners
In some asinine way
Turned in; turned out,
But you can bet you made hay!

Shitty grits,
Newest of trends
In a world of freaks
With their barnyard friends

In a world
Of deviant conformity
Two fathers
Equals
Two moms

Barnyard
Is
The bedroom
Bestiality
Has its charm

Kids,
The center of attention,
Sense "odd" love
And
See no harm
On their loving parents
They
Would never
Sound the alarm

Shitty grits
Newest trend
In a world of freaks
With their surrogate, foster, or adopted kiddy kin

Evil lives among us
In places we think safe
Just because "you" think it an "acceptable"
Home Sweet Home
Doesn't mean it's not debased

Seems no limit
As to what freaks will naturalize and do
How I wish
That was not true

SOMETHING NASTY

By Donald T. Williams

Like something nasty
Stuck on me and my shoes
No matter how hard I scrape
She holds my soul like glue

Something that you step in
Can soil your every step
Didn't heed the warning
Of how slippery when wet

Climbed the slippery slope,
Conquered the mountains so high,
Dived into the grassy valley,
And ravaged the dark territory less wide

Now, she's something nasty
Stuck on me as well as my shoes
No matter how I wash or walk
Something of her is left in the grooves

Something in her come hither wink
You know, the one without eyes
Has come to hypnotize me,
To love, loathe, prize, and despise

Now, the stink of her love
For me is so profound, so distinct
If I roam as true dogs do,
I feel my manhood shrink; that's not good; better see a shrink

But once around her
My, my, how it grows!
I dig ever deeper
As a fool digs for fool's gold

Like something nasty
Stuck on me and my shoes
No matter how hard I scrape
She holds my soul like glue

Is this to be the price of love
All fools of love must pay?
Can fools of love find their way home
Once from home, they've strayed?

KNOW DOUBT?

By Donald T. Williams

Was I delusional?
Cracked up
And
Wet?
Driven to insanity
Or
As foolish
As one can get?

Set up
By some street hustler,
___'_ pimp
And
My killjoy
Do my __ despise me?
I robbed their joy as boys?

God has all the answers
Guess I'll have to wait and see
Now,
The chips fall where they may,
And
What will be will be

Pain can be a blessing
Hurt doesn't mean the worse
Only my afflictions
In coarse words,
I do curse

Highest of order,
Bipolar disorder
A rollercoaster's
Speed,
Highs,
And
Lows

Schizophrenic personalities
Of man versus boy
Compassion for humanity
Null and void

Pent-up anger
And a need for well-spent shells
Seeing a "White Devil" defile
The sweet ___ I once held
Amounts to a living Hell

This "sticky" situation
Was most traumatic for me
Why she submitted to it
Is an absolute mystery?

How will I ever
Conquer the inner conflict in me,
Live in forgiveness
Without the vengeance I need?

How she still "star screams" in Triple X freak shows
For the Devil's minions' glee!
How am I responsible
For what has come to be?

These are frequent questions
An abandoned _____ must ask
Do I take an eye for an eye
Or forgive as God, by command, has asked?

As answer to my own question:
Live as peaceful as I can,
But living without my true love
Leaves incomplete the man

God has all the answers
Guess I'll have to wait and see
Now, the chips fall where they may,
And what will be, will be

IT'S ENOUGH

By Donald T. Williams

It's not enough
To use my love for you against me
It's not enough
To reject my need for you in bed

It's not enough
To work me like a beast of burden
It's not enough
To write me off as the living dead

It's not enough
To let pimps hustle me and pimp you
It's not enough
To "star" in XXX DVD's

It's not enough
To emasculate your loving _____
It's not enough
To humiliate so publicly

Now, that we are _____
Now, your decades of lies
No longer need to be said
To the ways of a wicked woman
No "good" man need or should be wed

You have received everything
You have taken even more
God not dog is man's best friend
Women are butt bitches
Proven greedy whores
On all fours!

Donald T. Williams

_____ of your _____,
Bearer of your "good" name
Better half of mankind,
Marrow of "your" rib they came?

Why then, would you betray me?
Break the trust and vows we made?
Why then, would you forsake me?
And wish for me an early grave?

It's not enough
To use
My love for you against me
It's not enough
To reject
My need for you in bed

It's not enough
To work
Me like a beast of burden
It's not enough
To write
Me off as the living dead

It's not enough
To see and hear
You scream
While __ fucked

It's not enough
To see you split,
Spit
And then,
Proceed
To give more head

238

I'm so better off
Without you
For with you,
What have I gained
And
Retained,

The promise
To pay
You even more money
And
To live
With all the pain?

No.
I was granted
Peace
The day the Lamb
Called me by name

"May you live well and prosper"
May your treachery
Not be a 'Trek" that's vain
Keep all our meager wealth
And
Your bragging rights
But
Give me back my "good" name

It's enough
To have used
My love for you against me
It's enough
To have rejected
My need for you in bed

It's enough
To have worked
Me like a beast of burden
It's enough
To write
Me off as dead

Is this
How I must feel
Having lost
Half the value of my precious days?

The price of love
Is costly
All
Fools
Of love
Must pay

When love is true and tender,
And not
That of impersonal,
Triple X,
Rough sex,
And
S and M lust,

Is it not satisfactory?

Is it not enough?

CUD

By Donald T. Williams

Cursing all day
Like no tomorrow
Living with pain
But to Hell with sorrow

Long has passed
The day we met
Time to forgive
Time to forget

The day we spoke
The day we kissed
The day fate decided
We'd separately exist

So,
So be it!
If that's what you want,
Why linger still to vex, taunt, and haunt?

Worked for so long
As you collected my sweat
Enough for an ocean
So many fish in the net

Cursing all day
Like no tomorrow
Helped pay our way
Paid back the borrowed

Guess what I received
In return,
Spit in the face
Which like acid burned?

Happy Days
What a memorable show!
Like reruns, are here again,
But as you already know

Females rarely enter my door
Are they banned forever more?
What can be such wicked trickery as this?
Had the witch, the She Devil, lived right in my midst?

Cleverly disguised deception
Wrapped as feminine sweet
Unexpected sour bursts the mouth
With malevolent betrayal cloaked as Halloween treat

When that time
Of year comes round,
I can feel,
My heart does pound

Birthdays draw for her and me
Times can be unsettling
For another year ticks pass,
Yet we're not together at last

Who can master
Such annual defeat,
Who tricks eyes
Switches what we see?

Lives in fire
But never burns?
To palates tastes great
As stomachs turn?

Females rarely enter my door
Are they banned forever more?
Lover Boy's no secret now
Yet, for him,
Where is the cow?

Lover Boy's no secret
He's crystal clear
Yet, the female
Fails to draw near

Mystery's questions
Asked, answered, and unanswered of late
The First Seven Years is a long tale
To chase in circles as bait

But the reward
Oh, so great!
Love conquers all
Love overrules hate

Worthy sacrifice
Well-worth the wait
Patience moves the slow hands
On the timely mechanisms of fate

Cursing all day
Replaced by prayers
Hold fast the banister of hope
Climb life's crystal stairs

Dreams take stage
In tomorrow's play
Though unrehearsed
I know what to say

Chasing one's tale
Takes time; takes will
Seeing the play from Alpha to Omega
Can be an awesome thrill

Happily ever after, utopia's destination,
Is perhaps, the toughest fork in the road not ____
When I reach the end of it,
Pray joy replaces the pain and aching

Cursing all day
Like no tomorrow
Living with pain
But to Hell with sorrow

Ever blooming
Love's bouquet
Sweetens the fragrance
Of the gloomiest end of days

2,555 days are countable
Each night, you're one less away
Prayers are the words of wonder
Like the bread we eat every day

Never mind the counting
Let nature take its course
God sanctioned our marriage
We still have His endorse

Lover Boy's no secret
No secret are you
How do you chew cud
That belongs not only to you?

Cuddle seems appropriate
But nothing in life is fair
Cud will never go or stay down easily
When what is, was to be shared

Lover Boy's no secret
He's crystal clear
Yet, the female
Fails to draw near

Mystery's questions
Asked, answered, and unanswered of late
The First Seven Years is a long tale
To chase in circles as bait

But
The reward,
The reward
Oh, so sweet!
Love conquers all
Love knows no defeat

Happy Days
What a memorable show!
Reruns are here again
As you already know

Long has passed
The day we met
Time
To forgive
Or
Time
To forget?

Never mind the counting
Let nature take its course
God sanctioned our marriage
We still have
His
Endorse

PART SIX
LAWLESS OF THE LAND

EVIL RESIDENCE

By Donald T. Williams

Damnden Glen
And Grandnight Ridge,
Two Greensburro, NC residences
Where you don't want to live

Two crooked establishments
Two dens of thieves
Welcoming signs and smiles
Are designed to deceive

Sure, you're welcomed
To get ripped off there
Pretty female intake representatives
Well camouflage the snare

Once you've signed on the dotted line,
False witness and accusation they'll bear
Soon, you'll face ill leGal eviction
Soon, "false" arrest looms in the air

Find yourself on lockdown or
Involuntarily committed and defamed
Wrongly inflicted, afflicted, and bound
In some utterly contrived "criminal", civil claim

Picture yourself the portrait
Of an elaborate "rip-off" frame
Taken for your clothing, new furniture, electronics,
Four rides, your identity, credit, and name

Lessors, cops, CO's, lawyers, and judges
All "in on it" which makes it a "damn" shame
Curses on you all and unrestrained
Curses on you all and never in vain

If you doubt my claims
A little research is all you need
Check the public and "private" records
Paper and electronic trails will lead to their criminal deeds

Damnden Glen
And Grandnight Ridge
Two Greensburro, NC residences
Where you don't want to live

Two crooked establishments
Two dens of thieves
Welcoming signs and smiles
Are designed to deceive

The Devil has a home
Just beyond their gates
If you happen to live there,
May already be too late

Keep an eye on your neighbors
An even closer eye on those keeping the grounds
Lots of strange things
Going on, in, and around

Safe, gated communities
Simply don't exist
Especially when evil lets, abides, and resides
Within the gates and in your midst

Damnden Glen
And Grandnight Ridge
Two Greensburro, NC residences
Where you don't want to live

Sure, you're welcomed
To get ripped off there
Pretty female intake representatives
Well camouflage the snare

The Devil has a home
Just beyond their gates
If you happen to dwell as well,
May already be too late

Ever see porno
In a Daily Newspaper's
Full page, color advertisement sheets?
Caught a White man at a Grandnight Ridge garbage disposal
Dumping boxfuls in heaps

Grabbed a box
To examine thoroughly on my own
What I discovered, red pen circled, and/or yellow highlighted
Made even my "questionable" morality moan and groan

"Respectable" motherfuckers
Held up in the Devil's Den
Packed my car and trunk
Prepared to get in the wind

Went to see my "traffic ticket" lawyers in Fayfartville
Smithe, Trickey, Dumpster, Karpenter, and Kondlin, P.A.
Is their name,
But no matter,
Probably aren't men enough
To substantiate my claims

Told my wretched story about the XXX DVD,
The Judge, J B,
And the "Newspaper Porn"
From beginning to end

None of my "evidence"
When I indeed offered, did they care to see
Said, "You make us nervous;
Please leave."

Started to head north,
Like a runaway slave,
Like a Jewish refugee
Next thing,
I'm shackled and locked up
Mercy, mercy me!

Found myself on 23 and 1
Lockdown
With illegible bail bonds men numbers
And collect call numbers
They never take
Every days a nightmare,
Asleep
Or
Awake

Damnden Glen
And
Grandnight Ridge,
Two Greensburro, NC residences
Where you don't want to live

Two crooked establishment
Two dens of thieves
Welcoming sign and smiles
Are designed to deceive

The Devil has a home
Just beyond their gates
If you happen to live there,
With the damned,
It's already too late

TOLD YOU SO

By Donald T. Williams

Visualize a fireplace
With wheels beside your feet
Woman on the floor in the center
Toyota leather as her seat

Pictured advertisement,
A foreshadow of the fall,
Green demons hidden in the wheel spokes
Are what I peered and best recall

Artful decoration,
Perhaps a future speculation
Telling of ominous events
Which have undoubtedly happened since

Hence, my mind holds the answer
My mouth now lets it go
Those who know the secret
Know I told you so

What a "spooky" revelation!
An impromptu observation!
As I fix up my new place,
With a power I am faced

Caution to the wind is tossed
As I minimize the lost
Pretty "White" woman in a bind
Is the place herself she'll find

Price for wrong
Done unto me
Payback gift
A "bitch" surely

Spooky revelation!
What's next to come?
Those who stole my treasures
Are the sorriest ones

Yes, I speak in riddles
With answers crystal clear
Those who know the secret
Have good reason to fear

Gross circle of friends grows tighter
Like the noose around the neck
What you've learned of cruelty
Be the experience you get

Platinum, granite, mica
As lifeless as the dead
So shall be your offspring
There's a bounty on their heads

Precious things to toy with
As was this life of mine
Think what I dictate despicable,
A return of cruelty in kind

Know you wish I was playing
Know "damn well" that I am not
Know that Fucking Cheese game tokens
Have been purchased to fill the slot

"White bastard" in G R's management office told me,
"Not to worry, not to worry about "her"."
Confirmed my worst trepidations
Verified the fact I had inferred

Now, I'm giving forecasts
Hold or hang on every word
Toyota was just first of many
Leading the cliff bound, stampeding herd

Visualize a fireplace
With wheels beside your feet
Woman on the floor in the center
Toyota leather as her seat

Pictured advertisement,
A foreshadow of a fall,
Green demons hidden in the wheel spokes
What I peered and best recall

Artful
Decoration
Perhaps
A
Future
Speculation
Telling of ominous events
Which undoubtedly have happened
Since the advent of my new sense

Hence,
My mind holds the answer
Hence,
My mouth now lets it go

Those
Who know the secret's secretions
Know God well
I told you so

GUILTYFORD COUNTY'S NA

By Donald T. Williams

Guiltyford County's
Nationwide Allies
Was in full swing
During the 2007
NC spring

Guiltyford's Gestapo
And
People
Had it in for me
Said this Northern nigger
Was where he should not be

To tear Greensburro
A new one
Was a sure enough mission for me,
Looking for some Lil Scrappile rapper
Who had dealings with my ____
At or around A&T

Working hard on a CD,
Somehow, my _____ ___ got beat
Went to Greensburro to get ___' and "my ends"
And went there ready for business,
Packing plenty heat

Niggas may think I'm bullshitting,
But, niggers and crackers know this:
Donnie C don't take no shorts
Donnie C don't take no diss

Saw that young, poor postured nigga,
The blue ball cap lover,

Pictured on a sofa, slumped forward, edged of seat
On Lil Scrappile's '06-'07 CD cover
You know the one!
Who is that motherfucking son of a gun?

Standing there, off to my side,
Looking wide eyed
At my ghetto spectacle
With some Greensburro Gestapo
In front of the Management Office of Damnden Glen
I shouted at him and them
"I'm ____' father; Where the fuck are my ends?"

Looking scared,
This punk's eyes are glued to the ground
"Look at me when I'm talking to you, Bitch!
Hear every word,
Hear every sound!

Next thing,
I'm involuntarily committed
On ___'s far off, Fayfartville say
Ain't nobody safe
Not with this angry, armed, crack head nigger around anyway

I've got to get "my __'_ and my ends"
Is all I that know
You can keep that bitch;
Who needs a ___ that's an ass broken, lying, cheating, bitch of a
ho?

You can lock me up,
But this I do know
I'll be back for "my ends".
That's for sure

Like a wild tornado
Too smart,
A cyclone
Too psycho to contain,
I busted out of the ward
In minimal time

With minimal effort
Of my mouth and brains

Like a wild tornado
I touched down
Again,
Deep
In Greenburro's nasty White ass
Fucked her right then and there,
Out in the open,
On the public and private
Green, grassy grounds

Shook that White ass,
The grass, bushes, and trees so hard
Everybody,
White and Black,
Knew I was back and jet Black in town

White folks' blackball network
Didn't miss a beat
Marked my ride for discrimination
Made it hard to see and hit the streets

Changing cars like James Caan
In the movie known as Thief
Didn't help or matter
I was cop-stopped and Glocked
For any "good ole boy", fictitious beef

White eyes filled with anger
Stared anywhere and everywhere I'd go
Nothing but hatred for me
These hateful honkies loved to show

White eyes filled with anger
Nigga knew he was "all the rage"
Knew that it wouldn't be long
Before I'd find myself in another cage

Weather was getting warmer,
But all I got was "Freeze!"
Locked me up on bullshit gun charges
And then denied release

Hotels, Lessors, Merchants, Car Dealerships,
State Troopers, Sheriffs, and CO's
Public Defenders, Lawyers,
And Judges
All players with parts
In the "Get That Crazy, Crack Head Nigger!" Show
Greensburro's # 1 Clandestine, Cable TV Event";
"Don't y'all miss an episode.
Watch a nigger implode or explode
It's TV and White family time well spent;
Before the next full moon,
We're going to lock him up soon,
And there's no one to pay this nigger's bail or rent"

Even called me "Simon" on the local radio,
"A star is born" in Klan
TV and radio land,
But I acted like I didn't notice,
Played dumb like a "crack head" too smoked up, too stupid know

Tractor Trailer Trucks
Following me to and fro,
But that's not unusual,
Why would I notice?
On with the show!

White "fans" following me
All about the redneck, Greensburro town
Center of attention,
But I'm nobody's fool or anyone's clown

Locked up and ripped off
With no home or place to go
A Black, nigger CO told me I was "homeless"
Not to let the green grass grow

Under my feet in Greensburro
Or the emerald hills of Hypoint
If I walk the streets of these cracker barrel towns,
They'll bust me with or without a hammer or a joint

Southern hospitality,
The kind I was destined to write about one day
You can pull your draws up, White whore,
But seriously, don't expect Donnie C to pay

Donnie C
Is going to get his "ends"
From those rap loving niggas,
From poor White trash
And
From rich White trash too!
None of you literate or illiterate fellow Americans
Can ignore this shit
The "art" compels you
Regardless of how hard you may try
Or
Demand your kids not to partake of such "grey", black hearted
poetry
It does have merit
Surely, you can civilly agree

All of us, all of you
Are that big, terrible accident
Waiting to happen on purpose
Because there's evil and murder in us, in you

Keep hiding in the bushes,
"Grey ghost guerilla"
Take a shot at this nigger;
I dare say, "How dare you! I scare you!"

You see,
I may have a death wish
Like____
Since you __ fucked
That ex-___of mine

259

Kill me and then
It's all over
As in the end
Of time

Guiltyford County's
Nationwide Allies
Was in full swing
During the 2007
NC spring

Guiltyford's Gestapo
And
People
Had it in for me
Said this Northern nigger
Was where he should not be

Blowing the whistle on all this shit
Has got me in the crosshairs for a "hit"
Race war said to come any day
Bring it White man;
What the Devil is the delay?

Ripping this nigger off
For all he's got
Means you motherfuckers
Will all get ___

Taking me to play with
Won't be the last joke
Just keep watching the news
Many more good and plenty
Innocence
Doomed to get smoked

People going crazy,
Going wild,
Off the chain
That's what happens
When White male nurses

Try to "dope" a brother
When White jailors
Try to drive a brother insane

Poor White women
That's a dying breed
A fireplace took care of that
Placed your picture at its floor
Now, you ladies (bitches) are trapped

Won't be me
Who slays you
Poor White women,
You dying breed,
Look to your loving mate
Look to your loving seeds

Once set into motion
Triple eights know no reverse
Only one thing coming
Is much more
Followed by the worst
"Race wars
And
Riots
Suffice
To say such vile things, frightful things about our women,"
You say, "He "perhaps" as "Demon" has spoke,
As "Terror"
Dost death promote"

Maybe
You're not "that stupid"?
And honestly, I ain't heard a word or got a shot from Cupid
Told you before,
Donnie C
Is no joke!
But, he can't catch an arrow or a poke drawn from the long stroke!

When you see me coming,
Don't stop me for any bullshit
Donnie C's

A loose cannon
And
Will bite you like a pit

Test me if you care to
For your life,
You may neither value nor care
For any weapon formed against me
Stops the clock
None living will be spared

Come, my Lord
With the fire
Come, my Lord
With the fiery rain

No longer
Is the waiting
First blood
Is drawn again

Guiltyford County's
Nationwide Allies
Was in full swing
During the 2007
NC spring

Donnie C
Knows you're still watching
Camouflaged just over there
Haven't you any manners, "White, grey ghosts",
Know it's impolite to stalk and stare?

Know it's criminal to conspire
To hunt a Black man as prize,
Fun,
Or
Game
Sure, you think that's normal,
But that's why you're criminally and clinically insane

Just because you run the Country,
Commerce,
Governments,
Institutions,
Courts,
Prisons,
Hospitals,
And
Sanitariums
Doesn't mean you're on the ball

Donnie C
Observed your mind bending,
Ceiling drawings,
Strobe light moving,
Sexual images on the wall

Is not it criminal
To deliberately "drug" a detainee?
Is it not criminal
To attempt to drive a mentally ill detainee insane?

Sure, Hypoint Correctional
Gave it "a good ole boy" try;
Sure as hog or your brother-in-law's shit,
With Donnie C, they tried in vain

Criminally sane and hate inspired
Greensburro's rednecks wrongly conspired
To violate my Constitutional and Civil Rights,
Yet, I' going to get "my ends"
In "this racist" and my "rap game" fight

Plant a bull's eye on me
Niggers or "White grey ghost guerillas"
On the city's street and in a County Jail
Donnie C can't lose; he must prevail

Use
The Law as cover
Use
The Courts, you judicial crooks

Donnie C
Peeped your hole card on a prison cell's ceiling,
And you didn't see me look

"Sad Sack" motherfuckers,
Antiquated,
Comic clowns
In a uniform cartoon

Somebody's
Going to "draw down on you"
Buffoon,
Unjustified pencil lead,
Dead in the streets
By some hoodlum creep
May be a midnight cowboy
Queer, familiar at a barrister's watering hole,
A busy precinct embroiled like a Wild West saloon
By some trigger happy, shotgun packing goon
Or
A safe day, straight up, shoot 'em up
High noon

Guiltyford County's
Nationwide Allies
Was in full swing
During the 2007
NC spring

What you did was criminal
Extensive is your criminal ring
Donnie C has your number
Did you just hear your phone ring?

Let it ring;
Don't answer
Prognosis
Remains the same

Diagnosis:
Inoperable cancer:

No known drugs
Can ease the pain

Your hate will eat you up
Consume you,
Body
And
Soul,
From within

Like any good,
Malignant,
Contagion

Pass it on,
Pay it forward,
Or
Down the bloodline
To your kin

COPS AND ROBBERS

By Donald T. Williams

Sent a couple of brown boys
To kidnap me from Grandnight Ridge

That's a housing complex in Greensburro, NC
Where I used to live

Tried to settle down
After my bitch ex-___ barked and shared

She might see me
If I get established there

Still in love with her
And busted up by separation pains

Loving and hating her
Was driving me insane

Who exactly sent those brown boys
I really don't know

Nigga never had any beefs
With those brown brothers from Mexico

Making like they were gardeners,
We spoke and first I thought they were cool

Few days later, they try to grab me,
But my 9mm Lorcene slowed down those fools

Next, I got Greensburro Gestapo
All around my house

10 to 1 with hellfire rain
They're prepared to douse

But, before the lead shower could begin,
Opened my door and let those copsuckers in

Gave two gats, my knives, brass knuckles,
Bat, ax, and more

Since I cooperated with them, they too,
Soon backed off and left my door
Asked for and received
What I was told was a valid receipt

But a Black man can't trust Guiltyford cops
They are full of deceit

Two weeks later, I get stopped by
Some highway cop

Comes up with a bullshit transgression,
But that's the ruse for the stop

Tells me I got warrants for guns
And some domestic beef

Motherfuckers only locked me up
So they could be themselves, thieves

Ripped me off for all my brand new shit,
Three new cars, and a serious, Dodge "Ram Tough" Magnum truck

Had me in their clutches
And I knew I was really fucked

That's how they do niggers and niggas
In that White racist town

Same thing in a town called Hypoint, NC
But those motherfuckers are low, low, down

Donald T. Williams

Hypocrites serve on their bench
And niggers, especially, get no relief

Have poor brothers locked up for months and years
Over the simplest beef

Where the white sheets are kept
Is anyone's guess

Hope you ain't Black and live there
Just passing through is the best

Best to keep on moving
Just stop by like a guest

Once they lock you up, my nigga
You're in a sho nuff mess

GUILTYFORD COUNTY, NC

By Donald T. Williams

Guiltyford County, NC
Is a "Hell of a Place"
Ask most brothers or sisters living or imprisoned there,
And they'll call it a disgrace

Two or more brothers can't stand in one place
To talk, sing, or rap
Annoying cops have to harass, frisk, or arrest
Have to order you to scat

White folks got them thinking
Jail livin' and incarceration is a normal way of life
In and out the system so routinely
The CO's become your husband or wife

Bitchy, White Platoon Sergeant,
A low life Hypoint CO
Wouldn't allow my one free call
Even after the Judge told him so

Vicious, thieving Law Enforcement Officers
Conspired to steal all my shit,
Discovered I knew a few secrets,
Decided to bury me and it

First, I get a hawk nosed Triple K CO
"Pretending to be a Public Defender
Sees three White defendants before me
But, when it's my turn, he's got no legal time to render

Public Defender
And CO?
One White man was both,
And this I know

Public Defender
Is what he 'pretended' to be
Saw this hawk nosed SOB
Looking down on me

Gave me a stare
So I gave one back
Challenged me to look away
But I didn't crack

Grew up always looking people
Straight in the eyes
If you don't like what you see
Better walk on by

Bullshit Public Defender
Counseled three Whites before me
Spent precious legal time with them
They left somewhat relieved

When it came to my turn,
This 'Public Pretender" turned 180 degrees
This bastard whose eyes were dead
Said he didn't need to speak to me

"I'm done with him!"
"I'm done with him!"
Shouts he before ten words between us were said
Straightening out his tie reveals a neck scarlet red

"I'm done with him!"
Calls he to the other CO's
I protest this bullshit, redneck mess,
But off running he goes

Later, in my Video Court appearance
This "same lame" jackass appears
Judge is a confused, bamboozled fool
Because no data or court papers are there

I had filled an affidavit before
With a more hospitable White PD cat,
But the same, aforementioned, hawk nosed asshole I got
Doesn't know where it's "at"

Laughing, dropping folders,
And slapping knees
This Triple K motherfucker and his crony
Are as happy as can be

Fucking over niggers
Gives them so much joy
I'm every inch a Mister,
But they still want to call me boy

Unprepared and embarrassed ass backwards Judge
Doesn't know what to do
Gives me another court date
Says I'll have to stew

Orders I get to make a phone call,
Get bail and an attorney to 'rep' for me
CO Platoon Sergeant says, "Fuck that bitch!
She's got no authority."

Furious with anger
Over this racist shit
Popped a fit of Black Rage
And got locked down quick

Three weeks later,
Well, what do you know!
Hawk nosed motherfucker
Comes to the 23 and 1 dressed as a CO

Last time I saw this bitch
He was all suit and tie
Knew damn well with 'me'
This shit would never fly

On the 1 and 23
In a CO's uniform
Bastard's shocked to see me
Because he knows he's been caught "dead" wrong

Nervous as a honky at a Black Panther meeting
This bitch denies all my claims
Tells the other inmates I'm crazy
Something's wrong with my brains

But, this hawk nosed "Triple K" sack of shit
I'd know any day, anywhere
Same goes for the Platoon Sergeant and ass backwards Judges
As if anyone "really" cares?

If I'm crazy and lying, why did this honky CO/Public Pretender
Act so nervous and scared?
Left leg under his desk was shaking so violently
I was sure some ligaments and tendons he'd tear

Next time, they even had an Uncle Tom,
House nigger Judge in on this shit
Video Court again, but this fool without a clue
Can't figure out who or why I'm there, and acts like a nitwit

Sixty days later, an older, cranky, house nigger Judge
Thinks he's a king on his throne of a bench
SOB talking down to the common people
Like he's some "God" heaven sent

Ups my charge to a felony
Tells me I'm facing "time" times five
Clearly this power hungry house nigger
Was out of his white ass kissing mind

I can prove everything
Of which I say
Bet my bottom dollar
This shit still goes on today

If you think I'm lying,

Go on and call my bluff
Bastards will try to cover their tracks,
But it won't be enough

Hate you with a furor
The kind you moronic "American" Nazis like
When you fucked with Donnie C
You sho nuff picked a fight

Pity you niggas in Greensburro and Hypoint
Pity you niggas a lot
Fine people like you niggas can do better
Than living with pigs in slop

Guiltyford County, NC
Is a "Hell of a Place"
Everything is fine for you
If you're the White race

Black folks who also live there
Must do the best that they can
Some help to lock up their own brothers and sisters
To the delight of the White man

I repeat,
Guiltyford County, NC
Is a Hell of a Place
Blacks living or imprisoned there
Know it's a disgrace

Greensburro Gestapo,
The strong arm law,
Bum rush the brothers
Without probable cause

Filling the jails
Pays their bills
Gives Blacks a record;
Helps break their will

Same old story
In the modern Southern town
"Know your place, nigger!"
And that place is down

Guiltyford County, NC
Still a National disgrace
Sheets may be in the linen closet,
But it's still all about
Power,
Money,
Hate,
And
Race

NIGGER JUDGES

By Donald T. Williams

Black, nigger Judge
High lacky ass on his throne
"Uncle Tom Motherfucker"
Make up his every bone

Doing the White man's bidding
Is all this "coon" can do
Swimming in the justice sewers
Is disgustingly something he's used to

Jackass ridicules a child
Plainly in open court
Making jokes and jailing niggers
For him is human sport

When it comes to my turn,
Bitch ass can see, hear, and smell my pride
I'm looking at six months, "if" convicted,
But thirty months this bastard tries

Sticks me with a felony
On a misdemeanor charge
Public enemy like me
Must not remain at large

All part of a conspiracy
To lock me away
What I know could ruin "respectable" lives
And most certainly shorten my days

My, this sucks!
I'm about to get fucked!
Watch your heads; Better duck!
Donnie C's about to run amuck

This shit won't stop me
From speaking out in court
Standing up for myself
Is the best lesson my parents taught

Always been a no shit taking
Nigger at heart
Itchy trigger finger
And a razor that's sharp

So Southern Justice has got me
As my C and C Rights are eroded and fucked
Tides have turned against me
Now it's the worst of luck

What's luck got to do with it
When for you there lies the snare?
Crooked cops in law enforcement
Crooked, ass backwards Judges in high chairs

All because I caught _____'_ butt
And a "Dishonorable", wise cracking Black TV Judge
In a Triple X DVD
Getting sucked and fucked

My story stinks just as much
As these assholes do
None can call me a liar
They "all" know it's "all" true

Smelling themselves and their genitals
They know how much they reek,
But truth is something more powerful,
And the truth is what I speak

HITCH AND ITCH

By Donald T. Williams

BD Triple K betrayed me
Witch was not much of a trick
For a slick, White bitch
Supposedly, to be for me
As my lawyer, Yippee!
And therein, lies the hitch and the itch

Paid well for "good" counsel
But got fucked over
By yet, another dame
No matter what the color
Bitches are witches
All one and the same

All these legal eagles
His and her court criminal creeps
Of the same corrupt clan click
All just out to legally rob you,
Rip you off,
Then swiftly withdraw and quit

Female attorneys,
"Especially",
Can be a bitch
Legally dyed blondes
In stylish business suits
Cleverly conceal a black-haired evil witch

Take a logically good guess
Just where
Her flying broom stick
Could possibly be
No curve in her back
As far as I could see

Donald T. Williams

Working both sides
Plaintiff and Defense
Concealing the truth
For her makes profitable business sense
Mole nose in the air
And breaking aloof

Gutter rats are her next of kin,
And sewer rats know where she swims
Working both sides,
Concealing the truth,
Obvious lack of professional thoroughness,
Is all the undisputed proof

I've a crucial need
To ID BD Triple K
As courtroom clan corrupt
Stole my money
Surely of which, I didn't have much
Stole my money and betrayed my childlike trust

Par for the course,
As far as legal games are thrown as played
Complete truth never sees the light of day
What's the use?
Had about enough of this shit
Hate you with a passion and love every bit

Female attorneys
"Especially"
Can be a bitch
Legally dyed blondes
In stylish business suits
Cleverly conceal a black-haired evil witch

BD Triple K betrayed me
Witch was not much of a trick
For a slick, White bitch
Supposedly, to be for me,
As my lawyer, Yippee!
And therein, lies the hitch and the itch

All these legal eagles
His and her Court Criminal Creeps
Of the same Corrupt Clan Click
All just out to legally rob you,
Rip you off,
Then swiftly withdraw and quit

Leave you high and dry
No follow-up or parting advice
Only thing that's left behind
Are dead, fallen bleached blond black hairs
Crawling on the floor
Alive with lice

Gutter rats are her next of kin,
And sewer rats know where she swims
Working both sides,
Concealing the truth,
Obvious lack of professional thoroughness,
Is all the undisputed proof

And therein, lies the hitch and the itch
Therein, lies the corpse and the stench
Full fucking forensics and a do or die hard Irish cop
Can't put a stop
To the black robed, black magic Corrupt Court Clan's tricks,
But Grey Spectre will white-hot spotlight this shit

Top of the world, Don!
Top of the world!
You've got to crack the oyster
To get the pearl!

And therein,
Lies the hitch
To stop this itch
Grey Spectre will pull the switch
Cast a white-hot spotlight
On this wicked shit

FONDUE

By Donald T. Williams

Got a new Virginian lawyer
About to "rob" me too!
More trumped up gun charges and a failure to appear,
But I know how these pocket suckers do

Can't or won't leave a nigger alone
When there's easy money to be shaved
But careful with those whiskers on your throat
When "your" neck is raised

Can't or won't leave a nigger alone
So they contrive some bullshit beefs
Again, cops as armed robbers
Again, lawyers and judges as clandestine thieves

Just more fuel on the fire
Jumbo jet fuel gallons on the flames
You foul white meat folks will get yours too well done
And have only your selves to blame

2012 won't come late
Right on time with prime time Race Wars. Great!
Bearing too many for the good and plenty
Body bags of full blown, bad blood hate

You see, I've got nothing to lose
Except a shit load of crap
"Love to serve you, Sir
Enjoy my "anal appetizer" as a pre entrée pate snack

Do not worry, Miss
The main course is on its way,
Shooting back sitting ducks having a turkey shoot
Make an elegant fondue display."

Got a new Virginian lawyer
About to rob me too!
More trumped up gun charges and a failure to appear,
But I know how these pocket suckers do

Just more fuel on the fire
Jumbo jet fuel gallons on the eternal flames
You foul, white meat folks will get yours too well done
And have only your selves to blame

Heard revenge is a deep dish
Best served when it's served cold
Sorry, but my revenge is white-hot
Much too molten for any dish, bowl, or crucible to hold

Now, you've gotten me angry
And when so, I move with posthaste
Time will go much faster now
As "we" hurdle to "our" fate

Got a new Virginian lawyer
About to "rob" me too!
Legal eagles fly the coop
From my pocket
Straight to you

The eagle,
For you, has landed
Just as you crooks
Planned it

Bear false witness
If you must
In the root of all evil
Place your trust,

But I've something
"Prepared" for you
Favorite, tasty, deep dish
I call Fondue

DRIBBLE

By Donald T. Williams

Judge Slimy Dribble
Chewing tobacco tucked between gum and lip
Dispense "your" unkind kind of justice,
But your own Judgment Day comes quick

Terminal your cancer
Caught but one minute too late
Fines and court costs you levied
Make double heavy chains of weight

Shackled to your unfairness
Wearing yoke of enormous size
You cannot know Heaven
Not with your cold, snake eyes

Just like Jacob Marley
You'll haunt men as they dream
Devil Hounds so snarly
Love dear the way you scream

As they ravage
Ten toes,
Two feet,
Legs to the knees

Before you beg for mercy,
Just remember this
So filthy is your laundry
So lengthy is your list

You have given sparsely
You have one tight fist
Lifeline thrown before you
Does vanish in the mist

Lifelines in your palms
Gave you the longer days,
But such lines do end
Now, there's Hell to pay

On the timeless river, the one without lifeboats,
The one without lily pads or islands remote
Heavy chains are quick to sink
No hope is known to float

You, who served without honor,
You, who served only yourself importance and pride,
Your clock has run out on you
Time to close your beady eyes; bid you no bib but tacky bye

Since you ran a courtroom,
Maintained "unbalanced" scales,
Since you played Almighty,
But missed the spittoon pail

Slime is all around you,
Tacky are your feet,
Nasty is your front of shirt,
And your afterlife looks bleak

Judge Slimy Dribble
Chewing tobacco tucked between gum and lip
Dispense "your" unkind kind of justice,
But your own Judgment Day comes quick

Shackled to your unfairness
Wearing yoke of enormous size
You cannot know Heaven
As the egg on your face does fry

CAPITALISTIC CRIME

By Donald T. Williams

Monkey Paw Private Prison
Is a Handover Cage
With seventy percent Black occupancy
What a descriptive name!

Owed by three Judges
And a Judge's wife, I hear
No conflict of interest though
Handover Judges are "always" fair

Overdose of cops in Handover
Keep the "right White people" safe
True concern for the welfare of the Commonwealth
And not a question of race

Crime is definitely down there
Property values are up
Handover is the place to be
If you're the right color and have some bucks

If without a badge and/or a gun,
You'd better take great care
Hand over your freedom or your cash
Because they'll hold you there

Prison inmates are valuable commodities
They are stored and counted in dollars and cents
Lengthening their confinement
Pays for their jailers' food, clothing, cars, mortgages, and rent

Conflict of interest
"No way!" the judicial owners say,
"We provide a necessary community service;
All the Whites appreciate our locked down extended stay."

How many prisons like Monkey Paw
Are open for business across this "free" land?
Even if crime goes down,
There will still be the demand

To fill those cages with someone
Evil plans for the poor of any color will not be undone
The courts will not have mercy on us
As long as Judges own prisons and rule above us

Jailer Judges have a way
To keep the human pipeline flowing
Soon, you'll commit a crime
And have no way of knowing

With Big Brother ever watching,
With eager "Leave It to Beaver" cops ever stopping and Glocking
You will know "to well" what you're risking
For just being you and for existing

Monkey Paw Private Prison
Is a Handover Cage
With seventy percent Black occupancy
What a descriptive name!

Monkey Paw Private Prison
Is an American, shameful outrage
Loathsome, criminal example
Of "Capitalism" gone astray

Nasty business imprisoning others
As a means of legal tender
Nastier than when desperate borrowers
Become the slaves of the greedy lenders

Conflict of interest
And usury interest rates
Legally rob from others
To fill another's plate

Do private prisons

Solve a housing problem?
Keep some in our society gainfully employed?
Keep the less fortunate from ever evolving?

Monkey Paw Private Prison
Is a Handover Cage
With seventy percent Black occupancy
What a descriptive name!

PART SEVEN
BEG YOUR PARDON? NO EXCUSE

TRIPLE RIPPLE

By Donald T. Williams

As writings
Grow more prophetic
As pens
Bleed blood in pools
As word plays
Are deemed pathetic
As listen not
The fools

Triple Ripple
Oceans come to plunder
Triple Ripple
Storm clouds rain bolts and thunder
Triple Ripple
The bad seed grows wild
As the tumble weed
Rolls and twists
So goes the child

Cruel is the unequaled treatment
Rock and roll does the sediment
Steamed clams cook in sweltering sand
Like walking woods,
They march from sea floor to land

Silky seaweed succumbs to strain
Relinquished footholds
Surrender under pain
Uproot does the root
To the tune of thundering tubas
Oceans
No longer the place of life
For fish
Or
Men in scuba

Like the squirrel
Does love the trees
So the faithful Christian
Bends both knees
Like the reed
Bends in the wind
So the foolish,
Yearn what could have been

True,
The Muslim/Moslem
Grounds down
Bows to the East
True,
Unleavened bread
Remains flat
Minus yeast

It's a plus
When faith you have
It's a plus
When love you have grabbed
Held its heart
Close to thy breast
Stored its love
Within thy chest

If 180 degrees
Becomes the Mound
If the bloody battleground
Becomes flattened ground
All ears did hear the gavel pound,
The deafening,
Silent sound,
Of "Justice"
Slamming down

Bluebirds screech out warnings
As the cat below does prowl
Bluebirds screech out bombings
Before the cat's doomed dome is fouled

Droppings from blue skies
Drop from eagles
As from doves
All will say,
"Where is the loving God?"
All will say,
"Where is the love?"

Cry does the dove
Die does the love
Songbirds sing only the Blues
What is the use?
When missiles cruise,
There are no happy tunes

SAMS fly up
As skies the flashing flack
The vain,
Futile act
Is but snapping fire crack
Failing
To keep the once silent silo's mouth
From shouting back

When,
Not if,
Comes the awesome,
Atomic counterattack?
No time to look ahead
No time to look back

Rock and roll
Does the sediment
None but "One"
Can but won't impede the impediment

Steamed clams cooked
In sweltering sands
Like walking woods
March from seafloor to land

Stranger things
Further perturb the plot
As crabs rebel
And curse the pot

Triple Ripple
Pebble on the lake
Rings appear
When comes the quake

Fissures yawn
Beneath the sea
Add
To present miseries

Rewind Shakespeare's
Plays of old as told
Play with words
Both hot and cold

Curtain on the stage is closed,
But the actors were not told
Play they do the expired roles and parts
Words and actions they've come to know by heart

As writings grow more prophetic
As pins bleed blood in pools
As word plays are deemed pathetic
As listen not the waxed ears of fools

The rock child
Roars rudely, unruly out of turn
Tough love parents and elders smack mouths and bottoms
So the belligerent will well learn

Breaking "Super Bad"
Is said the unwise thing
Waking mad and bad
The hard day and hard times bring

The tongue can be a lover,
The tongue can hiss like a snake

The pen can be a peacemaker
The pen can foster hate

Honey drips so slowly
So thickly and so sweet
A condiment is vinegar
It's sour, straight taste never weak

Flippant
Is the serious work I do
I'm so full of passion
I'm so full of cruel

Compassionate
Is the furious work I do
I'm so full of righteous anger,
And I'll be nobody's fool

If I have a master,
Say, I have a soul left?
Grey Spectre is but one answer
To thoughts and questions written, unwritten, or of held breath

Yes,
I'm on a mission
Like a crack head of days gone by
I do get the "drugs" I want and crave,
But this is some "dope" you can't buy

As writings
Grow more prophetic
As pens
Bleed blood in pools
As word plays
Are deemed pathetic
As listen not
The fools

Like honey
I drip slowly
So thickly and so sweet

Like vinegar
I complement
Sharp,
Tart,
And
Never,
Ever,
Weak

Triple Ripple
Oceans come to plunder
Triple Ripple
Rolling war clouds
Rain bolts and thunder
Triple Ripple
Born the unruly child
Take your life
And crack a smile

Yes,
I'm on a mission
Writing hand moves as if piston
Under fluid pressure and conditioned
I move like a reciprocating engine

Giving back
Exactly what I got
Stacking all types of cheese
In undoable knots
Rat packs better not come around
I'm back from the dead,
Recycled life
From a compost of Holy Ground

Rewind Shakespeare's
Plays of old as told
Play with words
Both hot and cold
If I have a master,
Say,
I have a soul left?

Grey Spectre is but one answer
To thoughts and questions
Written,
Unwritten,
Or
Held of breath

You may think
Donnie C could use a lesson
In tact,
Respect,
And
Humility
With all due respect
To disrespect
Donnie C sincerely agrees
To disagree

So,
Do or don't
Call,
Visit or write
Comment, commend,
Bitch or gripe
I'll accept or reject
Each delivery
Individually
As is my God given right

Streams
The Grey Spectre
Haunting and disturbing
Ever
Watching and perturbing
So
Observant and unnerving

As writings
Grow more prophetic
As pens

Bleed blood in pools
As word plays
Are deemed pathetic
As listen not
The fools

Grey Spectre's love
Is relentless
In battles for innocence
Grey Spectre's methods
Are defenseless

When need be
Calls the waves
Tides break bad
Moon misbehaves

Triple Ripple
The thing of wonder
Triple Ripple
Tsunami's thunder
Triple Ripple
Pebble on the pond
Land that was
Now,
Is gone

Without land
On which to grow
Will the wild child seed
Cease to so?

REALLY!

By Donald T. Williams

Donnie C
Is what they call
Politically
Incorrect

One thing about that aspect
Is absolutely correct
Donnie C
"Really!"
Doesn't give a heck

DC
Doesn't give a shit
DC
Doesn't give a damn
DC
Doesn't give a now worthless, Abe Lincoln, Red Cent
Donnie C
Doesn't give a fuck about the "White man"

Actually,
Not worth an upper case
You upper class
Sons of Bitches
Sit upon your golden thrones
Piss, dump, turn, stoop, sniff, stir silver spoon,
And
Slowly sip

The Breakfast of Scoundrels
Wheat germ and fiber waste
Taste forever great
Invite your wife and children
With posthaste

Silver ladle
Fills each fine China bowl and plate

Strong
Remains the "right" White families
Who always dine together and never alone
Both Father and Mother,
Religiously,
Never skip grace,
But can't wait to lick the unholy, golden throne

"Children,
Where are your manners?
Feed our leftovers to our faithful dogs
Children,
Where are your manners?
Save the dog's scraps for our faithful hogs

Let the slaves go "close" to hungry
They deserve no food or any pay
All they need do is work for us
Until their dying days

Pay them
Nothing in life
Pay them
Nothing in death
Reparations,
A pipedream
Inhale deeply,
And for eternity,
Hold your breath

Even the majority of redskins,
Who we bid drink
And/or
Drug to death,
Know this game is fixed
Yet,
We can correctly expect
The "assholes"

To make and take
The sucker's bet"

DC
Doesn't give a shit
DC
Doesn't give a damn
DC
Doesn't give a near worthless Abe Lincoln,
Let alone a Buffalo plug Nickel
Donnie C
Doesn't give a fuck about the "White man"
Who keeps us in a pickle

Donnie C
Is what they call
Politically
Incorrect

One thing about that aspect
Is absolutely correct and fully in effect
Donnie C
"REALLY!"
Doesn't give a heck

About
How crimson your neck
About
How vicious or real your threats
About
How strong your cup of bitter tea
About
Your Tea Party of Hate Family Owned Brewery

If there be lines
Drawn in the sand,
There better be deep lines
Drawn to six feet your clan

If gang busters
You proclaim, profess, and report to be

Then RICO Laws
Better be distributed fairly and equally

Bust you "One"
And all "Affiliates"
Then bust you "All"
And "White man",
Don't you Dare Discriminate

Legally
Fuck the "System"
Masturbate
Bust a nut in your hands
And then
Offer the "needy"
A fair shake
Squeeze yet another fat cat,
White collar crime asshole,
You know,
The kind poor people of any color
Love to hate,
Through a needle's eye size loophole
While his high powered attorneys
Monetarily propagate
As they procrastinate

Donnie C
Is what they call
Politically
Incorrect

One thing about that aspect
Is absolutely, I dare say, "perfect"
Donnie C
"REALLY!"
Doesn't give a heck

DC
Doesn't give a shit
DC
Doesn't give a damn
DC

Doesn't give a Red Cent or Buffalo Nickel
DC
Fails the low income
And
Unemployed working man

Donnie C
Doesn't give a fuck
Or
A hockey puck
About the "old money" White man
Who thinks he can
Keep our necks at his sickle
And
US
In a pickle

Donnie C
Is what they call
Politically
Incorrect

One thing about that aspect
Is absolutely correct
Donnie C
"Really!"
Doesn't give a heck

LOW LEVEL
By Donald T. Williams

Dragged behind a truck
Lynched upon a tree
Battered about body and head
Shot twice in each knee

Gas doused and set afire
Body bound in razor wire
Wear a necktie of my tongue
Electrify me just for fun

These are all
Your dreams
Of me
Heap upon me misery

Know you love the name
"White Devil"
Know damn well
How low your level

All that bullshit
About a master race
Worried about Blacks, Browns, Jews, and Gays
Taking up space

Sharing a nation
You claim as yours
Festering blisters of hate
Are your open sores

There will never be
Any victory for you
Confederate Flags
Are_____ paper for _____

Double Bolts and Iron Crosses
A waste of ink
Just about as manly
As your prison pink

Bet you're fiercely angry
Over what I say
Smart-ass nigger
Won't behave

Attitude adjustment
Is what you need
Conspire bleeding of your countrymen
To protect your seedy, viciously crazed, delusional, self important,
breed

No one is better!
Will you ever get that?
Fighting another Civil War
Won't bring the "good ole days" back

Know you love the name
"White Devil"
Know damn well
How low your level

As before,
"Good" will fight back
Again, you'll loose
For "good" you lack

Side with evil
Place your trust
Save your seedy seed
With pure blood lust

As before,
"Good" will fight back
Again, you'll lose
For "good" you lack

Tell me, hater
What good are you
If hating and killing
Are the only things you can do?

Benefit to this beloved country?
Statesmen and symbols of White pride?
You live in a melting pot, White Stupidest!
Face a fact only "fools" deny

Tell me, hater
What good are you
If hating and killing
Are the "only" things you can do?
Join the Military
Join the Force
Practice
Perfect
Killing
At the "People's" cost?
My God,
You're lost!

THE RAID
By Donald T. Williams

Not one to let
Ex-African slave catchers and traders
Off the bloody hook
The Heavens did quake
When the innocent you took

Tribe on tribe
To the savage victor go the spoils
Spoils sold down the river, down to the ocean
Bound for a lifetime
Of separation, degradation, brutality, and toil

Families,
Bodies, lives,
Dreams, spirits, and souls
Traded for trinkets, textile, weapons
Iron, bronze, silver, or gold

Nothing worth the high price
Captured slaves dearly paid
Nothing worth the home life destroyed
Once caught off guard
When came the raid

Not one to let
Ex-African slave catchers and traders
Off the bloody hook
The Heavens did quake
When the innocent you took

Don't dare disparage Black African Americans as former slaves
Unfortunately inferior to the African Dynasty of you
Red, Black, and Green roots
Make our families' trees inherent

Intrinsic to the African earth from which they grew

Who
Knew his enemy to be a knave?

Who
Knew the ocean's watery grave?

Who
Knew nerve wrecking fear yet was brave?

Who
Knew his women and children were defiled, whored, bought, sold,
and enslaved?

Who
Knew in his heart, himself "not" meant to be "any" man's slave?

Oh my God!
How much time
Was spent
Working as a slave
And not receiving one red, blood stained cent!

Oh my God!
Plenty hangings, rapes, brutality, and cruelty received
Whips, stripes, and burns
Struck across innumerable Black backs
For over centuries without reprieve!

Not one to let
Ex-African slave catchers and traders
Off the bloody hook
The Heavens did quake
When the innocent you took

Nothing worth the high price
Captured slaves dearly paid
Nothing worth the home life destroyed
Once caught off guard
When came the raid

Who
Knew his God asks him to forgive
The terrible territorial thing
To rise and fly above it
When "clipped" were his wings?

Not one to let
Ex-African slave catchers and traders
Off the bloody hook
The Heavens did quake
When the innocent you took

Tribe on tribe
To the savage victor went the spoils
Spoils sold down the river, down to the ocean
Bound for a lifetime
Of separation, degradation, brutality, and toil

NOTHING BUT THE TRUTH

By Donald T. Williams

Reparations,
Forty acres,
And a mule

Are they ever coming?
What was earned and owed,
What is long, long overdue?

Virginian gubernatorial memory lapse
Of an undeniable fact
Better Black smack

Some common sense
Into "our" absent-minded Governor
For such witless, remissive crap

Governor of the "People" he has sworn. Sure, right
How callous can you be?
To speak or write of Civil War
And fail to mention Blacks like me?

Only reason prosperous White Virginians live lives without want
In well-developed estates, mansions, homes, and communities,
Own businesses,
Properties,
Farms,
Et cetera, so forth, and such
Is because their ancestors bought, sold, and stole the "valuable"
lives of Blacks

Only way you "own" them,
Ex-slave owner and "Master "of inhuman brutality, greed, and fear,
Is off the backs, blood, sweat, and tears
Of Blacks like us who are so "dear"

Guess what else "is" or "maybe"
Long, long overdue?
Perhaps bouquets of "forget-me-not"
Lovingly placed on the graves
Of "all" ex-slave owners like you
To remind all Black African Americans of what you and what we
owe you

Governor of the "People" he has sworn. Sure, right
How callous can you be?
To speak or write of Civil War
And fail to mention descendents of ex-slaves like me?

Confederate Flags, rags, and bandannas
Bleak reminders seen locally every day
Country battlefield reenactments
Can't or won't let the old days, like old soldiers, fade away

Privately owned jails
High bonds
And high bails
Sluggish courtroom snails now prevail

Survivalist camps
Vicious Tea Party rants
Those who can,
And those who can't

Much time has passed;
A Black President named,
But little has changed
Disenfranchised people never reign

American terrorist threat,
American Nazi plot,
Blacks must rally, not riot
Against our jailors' devious plots

Plots most depraved
To "somehow" re-enslave
Blacks in other new, innovatively unscrupulous ways
When the old ways fail to rejuvenate the "good old days"

Always
Making more coffins
Always
Building more prisons and jails

Cells made ready
By the time Black males reach grade three
Blatantly insidious form
Of local, low level White male job security

One or two "fortunate" Blacks and browns
May slip through the cracks and become "someone" in fact
Either way,
The deck is stacked

Stacked against you,
Those "the White man has predestined to fail and jail"
Those without Second Amendment weapons,
Those without bond or bail

How soon "you" forget:
The slave's free labor, "your" thankless "Fetch"!
The slave's overflowing, bitter sweat
"Your" hefty IOU's,
"Your" ever accruing, high interest, unpaid debt

The James River ran then
As it runs now;
Was discounting slaves and Blacks
A current, running joke cloaked as a rambling understatement in
your swearing in vows?

"You" got blood from a turnip
"You" got blood from a plow
"You've" got blood on your hands
Like Macbeth with his bloody crown

Is a bloodcurdling clot responsible?
Did it impair your neglectful brain?
I'd really feel sorry for you, "Boss",
But I have my own problems and pain

The James River ran then
As it runs now
Not green for St. Patrick's Day,
But soon scarlet any day now, wow!

Reparations,
Forty acres,
And a mule

Are they ever coming?
Precious items earned and owed?
Commodities long, long, overdue?

Virginian gubernatorial memory lapse
Fails to swear in an undeniable fact
Better Black smack

Some common sense
Into "our" absent-minded Governor "we" should ignore
For "his" witless, remissive crap

Governor of the "People" he has sworn. Sure, right.
How callous can you be?
To speak or write of Civil War I or II
And fail to mention Blacks like me?

Do you like forget-me-not
And the inside joke most rotten?
Do you know common sense and courtesy?
Have you forgotten?

Reparations
Preparation H
Pay your debt and respect to Blacks
Or get a double dose of unbridled hate, lovingly injected by Dr.
Fate

Do you like the forget-me-not?
Does your well to do family own a plot?
A brain blood clot could drop you on the spot
Poor but polite Blacks would gladly decorate the grave where you
rot

Always worked well
With the land
Plant you six feet deep
And above you stand

Reparations
Preparation H
Pay your debt and respect to Blacks
Or get a double dose of unbridled hate, lovingly injected by Dr.
Fate

Don't doubt
The Black African American's will
Don't doubt
The Black African American's skills

You and "old money rich" White Americans owe great wealth
Undoubtedly earned by Black African Americans' ancestors
Better rewrite
"Your" wills

Don't doubt
Our skills
Don't doubt
Our will

Pay your debt
Before even more than your ancestor's gore
Rises from the spirits and graves of the Black slaves
You chose to disrespectfully ignore

Level the playing field,
Give peace a chance,
Or ring the pugilist's bell
Step forth and dance

Winner takes all
In a Final Grudge Match
Still think "you" can just "take" what you want
With a slight, sleight of hand snatch?

He loves me?

311

He loves me not?
"You have long wronged Blacks
So, SOS!
Forget me not!

Which in our regard,
A handout does not help
That's like giving naïve, Native American Indians
Trinkets and beads for their lives, land, waters, and animal pelts
To keep your white eyes scalps from hanging from their lances
and belts

Blacks love casinos
Blacks love land and material things too!
Pay what you know you owe
Our patience is godly, love of country is true
But payment in full is long, long overdue

Govern of the "People" he has sworn. Sure, right.
How callous can you be?
To speak or write of Civil War
And fail to mention African American Blacks like me?

Calluses on my great-great grandparents' hands
Whips, cuts, bruises, and stripes across their bodies and backs
Better Black smack come common sense into the "Powers That
Be"
For such witless, remissive crap

CLOSED MIKE OPEN

By Donald T. Williams

"Cocaine crazed Nigger
Most feared in the South
Will kick in your door
Will ransack your house

Give our beloved White bitch
The long dick of her dreams
Churn more fresh butter
With each louder scream

Better lock him up
Save and do what you love
Kill two birds with one stone
Or use a high-powered slug

False propaganda,
Increased public fear,
Makes the racism "right"
Gives our White folks careers

Cocaine crazed Nigger
With some snow or a rock
Public Enemy Number One
With a waiting cell on D Block

Catch him with a gun,
Catch him dirty or not,
Just drop something on him
Judges always believe cops

Cocaine crazed Nigger
Most feared in the South
Will kick in your door
Will ransack your house

Donald T. Williams

Give our beloved White bitch
The long dick of her dreams
Churn more fresh butter
With each louder scream

Pollute the bloodline,
Even steal her away,
Just look around you
More half-breeds each day

Look at "our" beautiful White House
What a damn shame!
Forever violated and creamed off-white
With a half-breed's black blot and stain

Better set him up, line him up
Save and do what you love
Kill two birds with one stone
Or use a "magic" high-powered slug

You know there are plenty
Of other fallible "Oswalds" in this world
Find one angry enough about our dismal economy
Or driven mad because some nigger fucked and knocked up his
sweet White baby girl

False propaganda,
Increased public fear,
Makes our racism "White right!"
Before and after a consolatory beer

Cocaine crazed Nigger
Most feared in the South
Only "one" thing more fearsome:
A Nigger in "our" White House

Better set him up, line him up
Save and do what you love
Kill two birds with one stone
Or use a "magic" high-powered slug

Put his "damn name" on a building
Put his face and big ears on a coin
Name a politically correct scholarship or club after him
That only "mulatto mourners" can join

Rename or build a Super Highway
Name a National Holiday to boot too
"Pin it all" on a lone, radical gunman
With a personal beef and proclivity to shoot

Face the Nation can face the nation with familiar, unsettling TV news
Lay this political embarrassment to rest in Red, White, and Blue
Place the Nation on the edge, fully back, or clear out of its seat with grief and/or relief
Over a foreseeable and necessary historical repeat
Quickly vote in a pure WASP as "our" Commander and Chief

Cocaine crazed Nigger
Most feared in the South
Only one thing more fearsome:
A Nigger in "our" White House"

WARTIME

By Donald T. Williams

Orange carnage
Dropped from a Vietnamese sky
By a USA gang
On a "Death From Above" fly by

Bullets buzzing busily
Prepare mincemeat pies for grateful flies
Plenty blood for drink
Makes a feast for their big eyes

Nazi ovens gassing "jester-like" Jews
For inhumanity's sake
Open up the bowels of earth
To see how many dessert corpse cakes it takes

Dropped an "Atom" on the Japanese
For the "Pearl" they destroyed
Keep a nuclear arsenal at ready
And plenty WWIII "Doughboys" employed

Gave Iraq a serious smack,
Searched the country side wide for a coward's hide,
Unearthed a cornered rat,
Stretched his neck, and that was that

Afghans don't die easy
Time and wars have proven that
Russians had their turn and cracked
Now, it's our turn at bat

Afghans never lost a home game
And yes, the Pak has got their backs,
But can the US go home as losers?
Face another Vietnam fact?

Always "boo coo" boodle money
For the waging of war
Citizens can and will go hungry though
That's the pricey "state" of the poor and war

Terribly unfunny
How some things never change
Time and war stand still for no one,
And full breed dogs never have mange

Kennels full of cute kitties
As caged mutts lick their sores and wounds
Champion fighter pits are inevitably retired
As the Angel of Death's needles loom and consume

The breath of life
Once given each as a wondrous gift
Values sacred and honored
Unanchored, set adrift

Veterans march the streets
Vets' civilian contracts have been breached
Homeless shelters pay their rent
Soup kitchens know their scent and/or stench

Mistakes
Unintentional
Inadvertent
Bad luck
Do over's
Continuations
Bailouts
Sellouts
All cost us "Big Bucks"

Seams to never cease
Filthy suits worn daily, again and again
Stinky of seat,
Butts hold their press and permanent crease

Who am I to judge
Another Battle of the Grudge?
The American Aristocracy of English stock
May care to indulge?

If a battle royal
They deem fashionable,
Our young men and women must fight
Either formal, informal, or casual

Suit of Armor
Does fit well the aloof,
But always far from actual battle,
And always "State of the Art of War" bulletproof

Rules of engagement
Plays by the book
Rarely matter if you're a White, white collar crook
Or a white CIA spook

Honor and duty
Pirates' booty
Spoils of war
Settle a score

Terribly unfunny
How some things never change
Time and war stand still for no one
And full breed dogs never have mange

Dogs of War brave battle
Hounds of Hell bask in Hell
Open mouth graves crave fresh bodies
And anticipate their smells

Terribly unfunny
How some things, never change
Time and war stand still for no one,
And full breed dogs never have mange

CHARGE!

By Donald T. Williams

How and why
Do we have such "learned people"
With such hateful dispositions
Seated in high, powerful positions?

Blind Justices
With the senses of bats
A Congress and a Senate
Just an "elite pack" of rats who repeatedly fail to act

How and why
Should we allow them to continue to reign
When they trample our necks
And obviously, enjoy our pain?

Revolutionary road
We should patriotically charge up again
Kingdoms toppled once
Can surely be toppled again

Tear this "bureaucratic mess"
Top down and bottom up
So, you like the taste of the people's blood, you vampire rats?
How about we overfill our cups with what you have on tap?

Just as you overfill your government, business friends, and own
pockets
With the common, working man's hard earned and over taxed
cash
You've got the brass to dole out billion dollar bailouts to inflate
bankers' golden parachutes
While our mayonnaise jars and kid's piggy banks get smashed

Do the middle and lower classes outnumber the rich?
Do the unemployed and poor outnumber them too?

If banks "too big to fail" are "so poor" with big money, numbers,
and financial plunders,
One wonders what are destitute people with "zero" left to do?

"Let them eat cake" was once given as an aloof answer
And that cancer was "cut" out quick
How about we cut the head off of the snake,
Donkey, Elephant, Conservative, Liberal, Independent, or
capricious "Socialist", you pick?
Impale all on an American Flag pole or a hickory stick?

How and why
Do we have such "learned people"
With such hateful dispositions
Seated in such high positions?

Blind Justices
With the senses of bats
A Congress and a Senate
Just an "elite pack" of rats who repeatedly fail to act

How and why
Should we allow them to reign
When they trample our necks
And obviously, enjoy our pain?

Revolutionary road
We should charge patriotically up again
Kingdoms toppled once
Can surely be toppled again

Such "learned people"
Such hateful dispositions
Blatant and scandalous
Worthy of an "inquisition"

TEA TIME

By Donald T. Williams

A ton of lip service
With a side of kraut
Guess what the Tea Party Movement
Is all about?

Stirring up trouble
Well brewed and steamed
Kettles whistle hatred
With honey, lemon, sugar, or cream

Nothing hides the bitter taste
Of psychotic White supremacy
Elections, the waste of time and money
In our fanciful democracy

Disrupt our flakey, shaky government
Let our "elected" erected house of cards fall
Taking back what is "ours", America
Is the last fight for US all

Blacks still waiting
On forty acres and a mule
Black farmers still waiting
On a "settlement" long, long overdue

A capacity to do good
Is the nature
Of boyz and girlz
In the hood

They "will" fight
And act out
If you ignore
When they shout,

"Take your foot
Off our necks,
Don't you fools
Get it yet?"

Equal pieces of American pie for all
Or this country will boil
A hot cup of tea full of hate
Translates as break every tea set, glass, bowl, and plate

Wild Boyz wake from slumber
To discover their ancestral roots
White supremacy is no pipe dream
Time to cut the drink and drugs loose

Wounded Knee is still bleeding
You can't shut out the deceased cries,
"Tear out white eyes!
Tear mouths that lie!"

The time is right
For the war paint's stripes
There's a noble cause
For bears and claws

If "we" can't have it, share it too,
Neither will the "rich pale" so few
No more time wasted to negotiate
No more time killed with endless debate

Give it up now!
No need for a powwow
To the victims who have toiled
Goes the spoils of our foils

No longer will we kill ourselves in vain
In a seething, drug land boil
Socioeconomic contractions activate chemical change
It's "you" we shall embroil

Drugs and prisons
The source of derision
Makes no sense
What "Whites" call a criminal offense

Snowflakes, weeds, and crystals
Do cover the land
Is this not a plague or plot,
A conspiracy, or divine retribution most grand?

Backfire explosion?
Bore barrel blocked?
Knew not the consequences
Of trigger pulled on hammer half cocked?

Something must have gone awry
Too many "middle" and "above bored" Americans gave them a try?
Now, the "future" slips through your pale hands
As does the mule along the Rio Grande

Legalize?
Remove the stigma of crime?
Open your opportunistic eyes
Those who "want" drugs will always buy

People of color
All over the place
What's going to happen
To the White Stupidest Disaster Race?

Time for a Tea Party
Time to gather and shout
Rally the militia together
Before the food, fresh water shortages, and desert's drought

A ton of lip service
With a side of kraut
Guess what the Tea Party Movement
Is all about?

Donald T. Williams

Stirring up trouble
Well brewed and steamed
Kettles whistle hatred
With honey, lemon, sugar, or cream

Nothing hides the bitter taste
Of psychotic White supremacy
Elections, the waste of time and money
In our fanciful democracy

Disrupt our flakey, shaky government
Let our "elected" house of cards fall
Taking back what is "ours", "nonwhite" America
Is the last fight for US all

Human lives not worth
A peso or a plug nickel
The possibility of "White" American heads bowling down our
alleys
"Now" make it despicable

When the tables turn
And "your swine head" is on the plate
Tea Time can come
And Donnie C can't wait

Slice up this American pie EQUALLY
Before, or is it already too late?
China's waiting in the pork fried rice and fried chicken wings
With beaucoup IOU's, higher priced pork bellies, and even higher
interest rates

Tea anyone,
Tea for two,
How about a tea biscuit,
Make that two?

U SUCK

By Donald T. Williams

U S A
U SUCK
The Devil's private sector
Shun the good and call it better

Did you not receive the post
From the loving, giving Holy Host
Who gives your people more,
Gives your people more than most?

Made you a Great Democracy
Made you a "World Class Leader"
Granted you wealth, power, and favor
But still, you selfishly deceive

Prophetic letter
In letters black and red
Did you not read and obey
What God's Word says?

Did you not read the scarlet letters
Which are as sacred as the Son's blood?
Have you no fear
Of plague, pestilence, fire, famine, or flood?

Hear no cricket's conscience,
The warning whispers in your ear,
Hear only the bats, balls, pitches, and hits,
The deafening shouts of a World Series' cheer?

Even wooden puppets
Know better than that
If you understand crickets,
Take note, pay attention to that

Donald T. Williams

Even wooden puppets
Know better than that
At balls, bats, and wickets
It's not cricket to cheat

Neither
Is to take an Oath of Office
And then
Lie each time you speak

It's not cricket to cheat,
But
USA
U SUCK
When dishonesty rules the day

When rules of Commandments,
Chivalry,
Decency,
Or democratic civility are thrown away

"Win" only families with money and connections
The storied prize of probable political pretense
"Take" vows of Pomp and Circumstance to represent
The "People" without a clue or common sense

Up by the bootstraps Presidents
Can be dinosaur purple for all I care
Elections nothing but a pistachio in a shell game
Pinocchios mockingly placed in the pinnacle seat of an "it's a small
world" puppet's chair

Giving the "puppet master" lap dances
As the ventriloquist, orates from the prompter, and gleefully pulls
all the strings

Only God Almighty and the Devil
Know what depraved pleasure that brings

USA
U SUCK
The Devil's private sector
Shun the good and call it better

Day late and a dollar short on their Tithes
Lawful Christian citizens pay their share in taxes
Yet, with precision on April 15,
You annually stab them and others in their backs,
Wasting tax dollars in twin skyscraper stacks

Shuckin' and jivin'; fuckin' and connivin'
Looking busy at this and that
Senate, Congress and Presidents
Need a laxative for all their crap

Rats in the train tunnel
Rats on the Hill
Rats in both Houses
Expect the "People's" few bucks to pay their inflated salaries, "all" the bills, and National debt

Frivolous with our money
Bailout bankers driving GM cars on roads to nowhere
"Win" the pork belly earmark race after race
Wheels, bacon greased from the inside, how can honest folk keep pace?

USA
U SUCK
The Devil's private sector
Shun the good and call it better

Did you not receive the post
From the loving, giving, Holy Host
Who gives your people more
Gives your people more than most?

Made you a Great Democracy
Made you a "World Class Leader"
Granted you wealth, power, and favor
But still, you selfishly deceive

It's not cricket to cheat
It's not cricket to beat
The American people who believe in you
Who give "you" more than God is due
Even wooden political puppets
"Should know" better than that
Listen, understand, and do what crickets with a conscience say,
Take note, pay attention, and act

IN THE ZONA

By Donald T. Williams

Arizona
Hispanics
Sound the Alarm!
The Whites have panicked
Situation dire; nerves frazzled frantic

Arizona
Hispanic
National Alert:
SB1O Law passed is one-sided and slanted
Hispanic rights now revoked, ungranted

Arizona
Hispanics
Statewide Alert:
Stop all Hispanics for a "color" search
Arrest all Hispanics for speaking their language of birth

Arizona
Bean eaters are up to no good
Go back home is where they should
Tag them and bag them if you would
Exterminate with extreme prejudice for the common good

Poor Arizona
What else can you do?
Lock up any
And every Hispanic
Who doesn't look or sound as you?

Hispanic:
Better have your "documents"
On your person at "all" times
Catch you, Hispanic without your "papers"
Caught you committing a serious crime

Note:
"This" may start in America's AZ with too many Hispanics
As "This" started in Europe's Germany with its Jews
Ask any average African American Black man about "This"
And he can tell you what "he's" been through

Sound the Alarm!
The Whites have panicked
Situation dire; nerves frazzled frantic
Heaven help us!
What is next?
Ropes,
Trees,
And
Stretching
Necks?

Arizona:
"Spic" fits the description
As an illegal
Law Enforcement has the eyes
Of an eagle

Arizona:
"Brand" Hispanics
By type of food
Harass for fun
Or if in the mood

Arizona:
Rid the state
Of Hispanic scum
Weed them out
Round up each and every one

Arizona:
Spic and Span
The Arizona countryside white
Get out of the state and country
If your color and language aren't "right"

Poor Arizona
Has a problem with drugs, kidnappings, murders, and thugs
Just as bad
Or worse
Than the inner cities criminals love

Hispanics:
Ready yourselves
Steady your aim
The lives you "may" take
Won't be in vain

Time rolls back to yester years?
Tear ducts packed and in high gear?
Tables turned
On the true scum
Hunt the hunter for survival and self preservation

National Alert:
"Call to Arms" if you're not White
"Call to Arms" if "they" pick a fight
Mix our colors and don't thin the paint
White Devil's may be against us,
But we're backed by God, Jesus, Holy Spirit, Angels, and Saints

Arizona
Hispanics
Sound the Alarm!
The Whites have panicked
Situation dire; nerves frazzled frantic

Arizona
Hispanic
National Alert:
SBIO Law passed is one-sided and slanted
Hispanic rights now revoked, ungranted

Donald T. Williams

THE RIGHT WHITE OR BLUE COLLAR

By Donald T. Williams

Cops and robbers
Both poised with guns
Video games practice mayhem
Kids kill for skill, thrill, or fun
Multitude of weapons
Overt and/or discreet
Promises to our Allies and creditors
The only promises we keep

Cops and robbers
Both poised with guns
Ghettoes' blood diamonds
Uncut, unpolished
Still glisten in the sun
Believing we shall overcome
Black Anthem etched in every heart and brain
Alone won't soothe bigotry's awesome pain

We must look forward
We must look back
We are well aware
We are under attack
From those who "protect and serve"
To pay mortgages and bills
From those living among us
Who would steal, harm, and do ill

Never cease trying
Believe that you can
The rewards are much greater
Execute a sound plan
Check the glass half empty

Check again, it's half full
Bank accounts need not be empty
A 9 to 5 you need to pull

Daddy with a job
Mommy at home or with the same
Low 30 year fixed mortgage
For a nice home suited for growing pains
Plenty food on the table
Car gassed up or plugged in the garage
Doctor, dentist paid in full
Credit cards with a minimal charge

"Man, I got a record;
Those felonies ain't no joke!"
False arrests, DNA mistakes
Serve twenty years and get out on a miraculous, "scitech" break
Twenty million can't cover
The pain innocent brothers have been through
No way can you "square"
The "legitimate" wrongs that you do

Who's Big Brother watching?
Cameras and mikes in every place
Surely you can see "them"
Sneak peek and show their face
Check those at the Church Mission
Check those who Law Enforce
Check the Judge and Courtroom
Check their laptops, butt of course

If you are Big Brother,
Protecting us and Little Sis,
How can so many go beaten, raped, dead, or missing?
Are you "The Finest" as you proudly insist?
You "are" Big Brother
Cameras and mikes in every place
Surely you can see the criminal element
Sneak peek and show their face

Americans, God fearing

In Him, declare their trust
Yet, words printed have no meaning
If closed Bibles gather dust
For the poor, success means
Luck drawing the short straw
For the homeless, night's rest means
Sleeping on streets, not sheets or an abandoned home's floor

Cops and robbers catch the same case
Rich and poor are in the same class
Race and class should be ice cubes
Which in time, melt in a crystal glass
Blending and transforming
Still quenching is the drink
Check the glass half empty
It's fuller than you think

Say Big Brother,
Buddy can you spare a dime?
Jump-start the American poor and middle class economy
It's more than way past time
Tap your greatest treasure
They're chomping at the bit
American "fighters" need a shot in the arm
We can give and take a hit

Cops and robbers
White collar crimes
Good boys and good girls go bad
Because of hard money times
Building more and more jails
Means America fails
To live up to its creed
Failing those in dire need

Never cease trying
Believe that you can
The rewards are much greater
Execute a sounder plan
Check the glass half empty
Check again, it's half full

Bank accounts need not be empty
A business or 9 to 5 "We, the People" can pull!

Pay an acceptable, respectable wage
"Welfare" is not an apprentice's trade
Unemployment Insurance
Has no endurance

Make a college education,
A career,
A vocation,
An ambition,
A dream,
A purpose
Out of reach?

Make US
A
World Class
Failure
Who fails to teach and reap the produce
Our Family Trees
Can bear
If those who govern
Really give a damn and care

YOU'RE IN POOR HANDS

By Donald T. Williams

You're in poor hands
With Awl Snake
If not a superb driver,
Get dropped or a fucked up, inordinate rate

Doesn't matter
If you never cost them a fucking dime
They'll drop you when you need them most
And that's a God damned crime

Donnie C had been with them
For close to thirty years
Fuckers dropped me cold as ice
Because they had some bullshit fears

Thought I was a major risk
All my years of loyal patronage
With them simply didn't exist
Wasn't worth shit

Funny thing how a black eight ball
Seems to follow me from Southern town to town
Starting to make Donnie C feel like these stale saltines
Don't want his black ass around

Ran this nigga out of Fayefartville,
SStandford, Lombertin, Greensburro
And that low point,
Hypoint too

Good Lord, my fellow Americans
What's a loud, proud,
Take no redneck racist bullshit,
African American, "smart ass", Black man to do?

Drive with no license,
Registration,
Or insurance
Like you bastards want me to?

Every day, with or without provocation
Face the fate of arrest in this Nation
Following the spray, tase, and cuffs
Much used without hesitation or reservation

Chances increase
For the young male Black
Shot in the head
Shot in the back

Chances increase
For the young male Black
42 9mm full metal jacket attack
In the head and back

Went for a wallet
Thought it a gun
42 rounds in the doorway
Another innocent Black man is done

Every day, face the Uniformed Threat
Off duty Iron Crosses, the eager merchants of death
Be forewarned and don't forget
Like minded Awl Snake will pull your safety net

Lost my coverage
When I went astray
Rhyme or reason
Didn't matter they say

Obey the rules
Or sorely pay
Either way
I had my days

Donald T. Williams

Why
Insure the insurance risk?
If you fuck up,
You won't be missed

You're in poor hands with Awl Snake
The hands of immoral, mortal man
They'll drop you in an instant
And really don't give a damn

Donnie C never had a dream or nightmare
About being President
That hell of a job has been miraculously been filled,
And I hear it pays the rent

Really wish that smart brother
Much more than good luck
Hope he's got the natural instinct
To know when to duck

My name is Donald;
I know something about ducks
My name is Donald;
I know even the luckiest Black man sooner or later will run out of
luck

Insurance is necessary
Insurance costs bucks
And even if you pay,
You can still find yourself stuck

Hope and pray
No harm comes to our first Black President, man,
But just like any other "Negro", I mean President,
They'll "drop" you where you stand

Like him, I know haters
Will have it in for me
Just how much time do we have?
Well, that remains to be seen

So haters, take the shot
Or maybe not
So haters, do what you plot
Or maybe not

Black men are a target
Always in the scope
Commander and Chief a great achievement
So maybe, just maybe there's hope

You're in poor hands
With Awl Snake
If not a superb driver,
Get "dropped" or a fucked up, inordinate rate

Doesn't matter
If you never cost them a fucking dime
They'll drop you when you need them most,
And that's a God damned crime

Don't feel sorry for you
Really don't give a shit
Made yourself a target
And targets do get hit

Bull's eye like an asshole
Donnie C's bullets fly straight or curve
Your dumbass went and did it
Where did you get the nerve?

Hands down,
Awl Snake

IF ENOUGH

By Donald T. Williams

If enough White kids do it
Then the Man will make it legal
Can't give their own a record
Like a Bugsy Siegal

Look at all those brothers
Doing real hard time for crack
White boys caught with powder
Get some short time, if that

White man can run a brothel
In some states of our USA
Black dude run some ghetto whores
Be sure to put him away

Now White teens in Vermont
Like sexting on cell phones
They're bare ass teen White girls
So the Man wants to leave their White asses alone

To fill the jails with their kind
Would be a shame and a greater crime
Can't give them a record
You know the Man's justice ain't blind

If you be of color,
Off to jail you're sure to go
Prisons are a business
And the inventory can't be low

Donnie C did a little time
Greensburro Gestapo saw to that
Whole town had it in for me
And that's a true fact

Made me do six months
And had me destined for 2-1/2 years
Got my black ass out of their grasp
And got the hell out of there

Left behind a D Block
Chocked full of brothers galore
Most of us looked bad
White folks would call us an eyesore

Keeping so many CO's in work
Our community's got to be feeling real hurt
Got to hurt something fierce, something bad
Locking us up and keeping keys is what makes the White man glad

Justice is blind as bats flying sorties at night
Three blind mice have vision for what's black and what's white
Arizona Sheriff says he's enforcing the law,
But he's the biggest racist White man this country ever saw

But, if enough White kids do it
Then the White man will make it legal
Can't give too many of their own a record
Even if they're like a Bugsy Siegal

Times must be a changing
Because Bernie's finally in jail
Took him out his penthouse
And finally denied him his bail

Donald T. Williams

Hope they jail his bitch too
And snatch up all of her scratch
There was a time when a Jew bitch
Would never have to part with that

Heard they finally got Filly Spectre
After six long years
Killed a White girl with his gun
So he's going to shed some tears

Obama's in the White House
Are we free at last?
That's the 64 Trillion Dollar Question
I just had to ask

SLENDER THREAD

By Donald T. Williams

Are bull riders homos?
Each and every one in three?
Those who ride the longhorns longest,
Love the longest horn indeed?

Is Broke Back a Mountain
With a deep crevice splitting its peak?
Freakish quirk of nature
Like the movie and its release?

Never saw this feature
DVD never warranted a peek
Call me homophobic,
But go ahead, mainstream gays in tents and/or lesbians in sheets

Guess I'm just old fashioned,
And it pays to be that way
Don't care how you spin it
It's unnatural being gay

Guess you could say I'm jealous
Women settling for a wannabe "with a rubber dick"
Men may be dogs and some dicks gross,
But damn! That's some desperate, desperate shit

If two are a happy meal, that's the deal
Who am I to say?
McDonald's, Wendy's, Burger King, or KFC
Have it "your fucking way"

Damn you, Midnight Cowboy
For legitimizing this deviant shit
Hope Marion wasn't a Rock in the closet
Because I was sold on his True Grit

Where's this country going?
Ass backwards to where it's been?
Rooster's got cock burn for all those females
But never fucks a hen?

How in the heck
Do the hens keep laying?
Switch hitting roosters
Pitching, catching, fielding, and base playing

Being down on the farm
Has lost its rural charm
Hatcheries are the untreatable, inhumane craze
Pent up animals worse off than rats in a maze
Fastest way our food is "raised"
Who gives a rat's ass?
Where's my ham and eggs?

This fast paced life
Is time to halt
Mixed up youth
Is all our fault

What once played "only" in Hollywood
Is now the comedic/tragic theatre of everyday life
Man takes man as husband
Woman takes woman as wife

When the deviant becomes the norm,
When the pedophile means no harm,
How much can a Nation's fabric take
Before the threads of our society break?

Are bull riders homos?
Each and every one in three?
Cowboys were once my heroes
But is Sonny safe to sit on Grandpa Gabby's knee?

If two identical burgers or burgettes
Make one happy meal or deal each and every day,
Stands to reason, they're sappy happy together
And therefore, seal the deal as gay

The rest of us, happily out of step with the abnormal
Embrace the Orthodox as formal
So please, don't step in my normal way
Not on any given, sappy happy day. Okay?

How much
Can a Nation's fabric take
Before the threads
Of our society break?

Behind closed doors,
People will always do their own thing
Consummate a relation or marriage
With or without a ring

With or without paper permission,
With so many mutual's decisions,
Many think we "all" should envision
That one plus one equals any two; so why the division?

Questionable consensual decisions
Open the closet door for consequential derision
Don't ask; don't tell
Keep your dirty secrets; oust the closed closet smell!

More or less
Means leave normalized, today's standard civilized, deviates alone
Let them eat fish
Or suck on a bone

What's a tolerant, Nation's proud people to do
When "In God We Trust"
Are pearls of fiction
Far removed from a grain of truth?

With God out of the equation,
Then this forsaken Nation
Can evolve into a placation
Citizens null and void of supplication

Go ahead! Ride 'em cowboy!
Live life on and off the wall of a bathroom stall
King of Pop's proclamation, all the sensation,
Number 1 "free love" death call

Yet, we keep dancing
Moon walk on Holy Ground
Bass and back beat just beat it
As young and old hearts rhythmically pound

Rhythm of a nation
Buck wild and led astray
Without Commands, once out of hand
Law and order, like reruns, runs away

No one and nothing can be counted on
Male and/or female comfort the client, John
For now, a "privileged" civilization
Neutered, neutralized and long, long gone

Surely,
When and if anything goes
Anarchy's brass knuckled fists
Will undoubtedly break some cosmetic noses

Are bull riders homos?
Each and every one in three?
Those who ride the longhorns longest,
Love the longest horn indeed?

Is Broke Back a Mountain
With a deep crevice splitting its peak?
Freakish quirk of nature
Like the movie and its release?

Guess I'm just old fashioned,
And it pays to be that way
Don't care how you spin it
It's unnatural being gay

Damn you, Midnight Cowboy
For legitimizing the deviant shit
Hope Marion wasn't a Rock in the closet
Because I was sold on his True Grit

What once played "only" in Hollywood
Is now the comedic/tragic theatre of everyday life
Man takes man as husband
Woman takes woman as wife

When the deviant becomes the norm,
When the pedophile means no harm
How much can a Nation's fabric take
Before the threads of our society break?

Are bull riders homos?
Each and every one in three?
Cowboys were once my heroes,
But is Sonny or Bonny safe to sit on Grandpa's or Grandma's knee?

Race paced mixed message
Time to halt the assault
Mixed up youth facing turmoil
In a Nation cracking with faults

The Nation's virgin wool is at stake
Even the strongest of thread can break
Don't pretend he is a she
That is not how it should be

Twists and turns have brought us here
Straight and narrow I do cheer
Don't pretend a her a him
Good is good and sin is sin

Imperfections
Do allow
None is perfect
Do avow

This,
The reasonable will concede
Reconcile with God
The remedy

Keep God in the daily equation
God blesses the sacred Nation
Separate from land the tree
Be without the fruit for thee

"CHICAGO, MY KIND OF FROWN"

By Donald T. Williams

Kill yourselves niggas
One shot at a time
Kill yourselves niggers
Take a life and pay it no mind

Just another nigga
Bleeding out in the streets
Seven days pass
Another 7 niggers dead in a week

Sign of the times?
No. Just the same old thing
Niggers know the night before
What the next day could bring

Today's young niggers
Are pretty quick with the beat or the heat
Niggas never back down
Niggers never retreat

All depends on what you're throwing
In this crapshoot we call life
Snakes eyes aren't good looking
Seven and eleven are very nice dice

Lucky shooters who make it
Pass the ghetto gauntlet
Of incest, prostitution, ignorance,
Drugs, guns, knives, fists, and knocking boots

Somehow, get an excellent education
Somehow, get a well paying government gig
Somehow, get to lead a nation
Somehow, get it back on track and off the skids

Hope this broke ass country
Still has its own horn to toot
Hope our ass backward government officials
Can get things straight, wise up, and give a hoot

If not,
Stop killing yourselves niggas
Make Top Prize and
SUPERSIZE a young nigga's long life

If you've got to __ someone, nigga
Make sure he's a "dirty, corrupt cop!"
Filthily covered in corruption's and racism's slop
Never mind his color, it he's dirty, take the __!

Do it now niggers!
Before "they" get all our guns
Out of our hands, homes, and off our streets
Empty hands are the hands most weak

Deputies, Sheriffs, State Troopers too,
Detectives, Officers, Captains, and C.O.'s who
Pretend to be a law abiding some ones they're not
Deserve nothing less than to be __ and forgot

Fuck you!
____ you!
Forget you!
Twice as fast as you'd shoot and forget me

Drape the coffins
Twenty one guns salute
Trumpets break wind, have a blast
Now the graves eat their fruits

Do it now, niggas!
You don't need to see no white fucking sheets
To know their hate for you
Their love to see your blood in the streets

Even out the killing fields
Equalize the deaths and misery
Know now the impossible is possible
Rewrite, write your own history

Am I inciting riot, civil unrest,
Or a terrorist threat?
Nope. Donnie C's a lover;
The streets aren't Valentine red and wet enough yet

Kill yourselves niggers
One shot at a time
Ammunitions getting harder to get
Some shells you can't even find

Chicago, Chicago
Still, my kind of frown
If we can't shoot you,
We will beat you down

PJ MAC

By Donald T. Williams

News is Poppa Johnson
Had ten years of sticking Daddy dick
To his baby girl named Mac
Ten years of triple X access
And her baby girl pink tongue for his sack

Mare mouth now neighs
She was down and cool with all that
Poppa's hippie rhythm
Put real swing in his bat

Poppa hit Mac's sweet spot
Two or three times a night
Being rich, famous, freaky, and high
Must have given Poppa J. the wood and the right

"Keep it in the family"
Must be the deviate family man's dream
Can't tell the difference
Between a child's smile, cry, or scream

Goes to show
Adult and child stars
Can fall to new lows
In those Hollywood Heights

Fact is
Everyday suburban, urban, and rural
Children
Face the same pervasive and disturbing plight

Incest is a way of life
For more and more "family guys" it seems
Sex kids don't get a chance to mature
Before smeared with Daddy's cream

What's done in the dark
Comes out in the light
Raping your kids is wrong
Be you red, brown, black, yellow, or white

Getting your jollies
Must not be a need so strong
That Poppa becomes a monster
His child's kin and King Kong

Old News is Roman's genitals were burning
With lust for a sweet ass thirteen
She was just the right age and size
For the dwarf director with plenty green

Time has passed
The child has recovered, grown, adjusted
And long been paid
Roman's due his accolades and props
So why is this old story news today?

Seems a pedophile back then
Is still a pedophile today
And just because Roman ran
Doesn't mean Roman will really get away

Time to bust your ass, Roman
The same way you once did
Hope your last days are tightly uncomfortable
When you finally do your bid

But that will never happen, Big Shot
Too White, too rich for that!
Why put Roman in prison?
Leave room for another Black

FATHER'S DAY

By Donald T. Williams

Father's Day is a blessed day
No more or less important
Than the day after or before

Some think
Being a father is an honor
Some think
Being a father is a thankless chore

Others think
Being a father is a lengthy prison sentence
Unwanted children were unfortunately born
As a sexual conquest to be explored and
Then consequently ignored

Why bear
Eighteen years or more of unbearable hard time
With only one unworthy woman
And confined to a cell called home?

Why be
Forever tethered by marriage
To a valueless and ungrateful family?

Leaving the busty mountains
Tender lush valleys
And the musk of the lusty range not roamed?

Irreverent pearls
Cast before
Irrelevant swine

Certainly, no need for concern
Certainly, not worthy of a "man's" time

Father's Day is a blessed day
Regardless and nonetheless

Some "don't" do what they can
Some do only their very, very best

Take them or leave them
Love them or grieve them
As is done
With the children they bear

This world is stuck with the lot
Stuck with the seeds cherished
Stuck with the seeds forgot

Commit the crime
Enjoy the sublime
Then accuse and deny
You can't blame the "set up" guy

Today's women are so sneaky and sly
Beside you, they always have "a woman"
And two or three "booty call" dudes
On the side

In the sex and quasi-love gone astray
Life style of tomorrow here today

Forget the old fashioned formality of foreplay
It's simply play or get played

Lesbian couple offers you a three way
And you say, "Man, I mean "ladies",
That sounds freaky great!"

Got you crushed in between their body sandwich
And your hot dog's "mayoed" coming out the gate?

355

Your greyhound's chasing rabbits in a race
He can't possibly win
Popped the cork like well-shaken champagne,
But can a hot dog like you do that magic
Again?

You're the one or two trick pony on this
Merry go round
And the brass ring is to fill the rabbit hole
With your creamy seed

Ride once
Ride twice
Ride thrice
Should do the gooey deed my handsome steed

Having served your purpose for these two lovers
Things cool down
The room soon grows cold without delay

"Sure was nice to have ridden you
Now, would you please get out and
Be on your way

Your dumbfounded look
Is so pathetically adorable
But please cut the act
You knew from the jump and before the bump
That the two of us were obviously gay

Perhaps child support and a bimonthly
Visit
May be the only manly or fatherly dues
You'll ever have to pay

And by the way, never play, just pay
Remember, we're a happy family and
We're happily gay"

Good thing child support
Stands like a three legged broken stool

The checks will always be in or with
The mail male
If you believe that my female fools
With your strap-on tools

Father's Day is a blessed day
No more or less important
Than the day after or before

Genuine sons, daughters, and mothers
May decide to pour
A thimble full and no more
Of their precious love

Upon the male who fills the fictitious
Head of the household, "Boss Man's" seat

The one who rules the roost
Now, that's one great feat
King of his castle
Lion's share on every plate

These are long lost masculine daydreams
Given up and lost among the litter

As the little one's needs grow and exceed
They randomly inflate or deflate
The egos and dreams of bigger
Or lesser men

Fine Fathers find a way to "man up"
And win
In the face of good times
And in the face of the grim

They stand tall and firm
On what's within

The very seeds from which
A family can only begin

357

Donald T. Williams

Father's please
Be fathers

Be fathers for good
Be fathers right now

If you can't be a good father
Then, "damn it", don't
Don't milk the cow

But, dogs like me, dogs like you
Can be bull headed
So head strong
Can't anybody advise them
On what they should or shouldn't do

Bulls and cows were made to breed
And each have natural needs

So what's a dog going to do?
Be a man and a father, dog

MOTHER'S DAY

By Donald T. Williams

Take it from a son, a brother, a husband, a father
Who knows
You can't trust
Not one of them ho's

Take it from a son, a brother, a husband, a father
Shot down to the flo'
Those ho's will take all
And look for more

Finding a woman
You can "truly" trust
Is harder than stopping
A Pittsburg Bus

Most people know that cheating game
Is a crowded, two way street,
How many know
A preacher's daughter's deceit?

Quiet, demure, absolute fake
'Tis the dark tempest as "white" snowflake
Purity and decency laid to waste
Path of destruction in her wake

None the wiser
Is the fool
Her lying lips
Make his lips drool

Such was I
There's no pretend
'Tis my tortured heart
I hope to mend

Female flakes
Are the creepiest female freaks
When the snake slides cross the floor,
You never hear it creak

You can't turn a whore into a housewife
Is something most brothers know
What I've learned the hard way
Is that your wholesome _____ can turn into a horrendous ho

How she comes to be that way
May or may not be your own fault
When the bitch is turned out and gone,
What was yours comes under serious and most vicious street
assault

All the dogs can smell her
There's no end to the train or line
All they know is the meat's fresh
And fine, fresh meat is quite a find!

Standing up,
Laying down,
On all fours

Mouth,
Pussy,
Ass

All an inviting,
Open door
Of the willing whore

Bitch will walk in your own home and say,
"I got a messed up cootie,
But not to worry,
I'll be just fine
Must work late "again" tomorrow, honey; this job blows and can
be such a grind,
Be home late,
About the same time."

Trust one
If you want to

Trust one
If you must

But "trust" no farther
Than you can hurl a Pittsburg Bus

Forget Me Not
She is not
One to trust
With your heart,
With all you've got

She's a bitch
Prone to heat and lust,

Even if you bust
Your best load

Like a bio diesel powered
Pittsburg Bus

She's a bitch
NO man with sense trusts

Mothers,
Sisters,
Daughters,
Too!

Wifeys,
Homemakers,
And
Goodie two shoes

Aunties,
Nieces,
And cousins
Who

Have the "V"
Do share the name
Bitch and dog
Are both the same

This unflattering clarification
Proven true to me
Was made quite apparent
By my conniving, Triple X _____

If, for some reason,
I have been in ere,
You can talk to me, "Sweet Baby June"
You should clear the air

Don't feel sorry for you
Really don't give a shit
Made yourself a target
And targets do get hit

HELENA YES! HELENA NO!

By Donald T. Williams

Helena, Montana,
What a moral shame!
Suggesting
To teach five year olds about sex
Is
Clearly insane

Encourage them to decide
If they're straight or gay?
Explore the world of sex
Even if the sex act's depraved?

Is this the proper way
To prepare our youth?
Chuck the English, Math, Science, Phys. Ed. And Art
But give Sex Ed. A boost?

Bullies across the nation
Do give pause to think
Kiddies committing suicide
Surely "did" need a shrink

Five year olds shoving sticks
Where they don't belong
Teen boys beating and controlling teen girlfriends
Because it makes them feel strong

Day late and a dollar short
Perhaps
We better not
Pause
Early Sex Ed.

Donald T. Williams

And
Anti Bullying
May be a noble
Cause

Oral sex
Is a way of saying yes and no?
Anal sex
Is okay because a baby,
In the shitty place,
Won't grow?

Sexting
Is an uncool,
Cool way
To make use of your thumbs?
Video
Your roommate's sex play
Send the shots when he/she comes?

Pandora's Box
Is a box that's better left closed?
How soon is too soon
For carnal knowledge to be known?

Bullying
Is a physical and emotional crime
What's your opinion on this fact?
Must another child self destruct
Before we, as adults, act?

Helena, Montana,
What a moral shame!
Suggesting
To teach five year olds about sex
Is
Clearly insane

Kids are growing up fast
This none can deny
We can't let them run amuck
We at least must try

To equip them with "good" knowledge
The kind from which sound character grows
To us they look for right and wrong
But what's the "most" that we show?

A little knowledge is dangerous
No knowledge is a greater ill
Too much knowledge too soon
Can be a tightrope or razor's edge at your will

Some may say,
"You failed as a parent!
Crack head teacher,
How little did you know!"

Years have passed,
And I'm free at last
There's a slim chance
Some wisdom will show

Which is what is needed
When dealing with children as delicate as ours
Bullies need not be bullies
If they didn't "already" have their scars

Bullies across the nation
Do give pause to think
Kiddies committing suicide
Surely "did" need a shrink

Day late and a dollar short
Perhaps
We better not
Pause
Early Sex Ed.
And
Anti Bullying
May be a noble,
Necessary
Cause

PART EIGHT
MUST I STAND ALONE?

BUT BY THE POWER
SO BLACK, SO BOLD, SO BEAUTIFUL: FM 88.8
DONNIE C's CREW

BUT BY THE POWER

By Donald T. Williams

But
By the power
He
Has given me
Powerless
In every way
Shaped
In His very image,
The living,
Breathing clay

Keeper
Of this green earth
Covered
In mostly blue
He
Would not destroy it
Nor
Would He kill its fruit
Tree of life, long planted
Deep rooted, as broad as tall
Woodsmen
Never touch it
No ax
Can make it fall

Why then
Do axes decimate the green place?
Why then
Do major miners,
Like acne,
Pot mark a pretty face?
Why then
Do oil riggers

Knowingly,
Commit disastrous environmental crimes,
Shaving time?

At crucial times
So careless in their ways
Waste the precious black crude
The Dragon's flesh has made?
Stored below the surface,
Secreted, safe and sound
Up the pipe comes thunder
Pure lightning from the ground
Now we face the music
As the piper's flute gushes sweet crude's sound
Regret to have spilled the chocolate milk of industry we have
found

Resting place of Dragons
Disturbed from slumbered sleep
Now, the time for crying without drying
As rivers of tears run oceans deep
Begging for forgiveness
Is the "tick tock" too late,
Broken
Are the hinges on the Dragon's unholy gate?
Hunger feasts on famine
So plump are men of sin
Plenty for the eating
Becomes one's next of kin

Bacon fat of swine flu
Burnt and smoking
Swollen Sun,
The yellow yoke,
Fries near
Air is but for choking
Man smells the putrid smoke
Putrefied
All matter that matters
Scatters
As evil walks all earth

Man and the abortion,
The butcher's style of birth,
Flourishes
As each disposable lovechild is torn away
Deathday candles light its way
To the unmarked grave or dumpster where it and others will lay
Until they're called to rise one day

Now that you are happy
And sodomized the child,
Doubles are your pleasures
Troubled are your sad smiles
Coming to your senses,
Reality undone,
You have not seen Jesus
Unholy is first one
Count upon your fingers
The syllables of song
Triple check your accuracy
Pray your calculations not wrong

Triple check your answers
So six the sick can be!
When you only count them,
And yet, you fail to see!
Only "One" before you
"Triple Cross", "Trinity", "The True Three"
Math and your computers
Still hide the mystery
Simple Simon knows them
His name is Donnie C
Silver tongue swift tricky
Streaks truth like lies mercury

Know sincere my Master
Who holds the only key
Confess your wrongs to Him,
Not me
In His love,
Be thy mercy
If faith is of thee

Students of the dark arts
Spanish cocker spaniels
With your traps and your snares,
Frighten me with silence?
Read this and "then" despair

Spanish cocker spaniels,
Developed English breed
Drooping ears are antennae
Still, you fools do not heed
Cry satanic Anatnas' guitar
Your cries do please my ears
As does Standard English
The language that you fear
Speak the King's English
The language we hold dear

Spanish cocker spaniels,
Slippery water snakes
Think they make earth rumble,
Think they make the earth quake
Foolish is the Devil
In his furnace here or below
He knows not of glitter?
All that shines is not gold
Frighten me with silence?
Emboldened is my soul!
Multiply the virgins
By the evil done by you
Come His true blue Horsemen
Ride hard, they come for you
Can you solve the riddle?
What has center
Yet, no middle?

Know well the mysteries?
Study the Black Magic?
Read palms to steal the purse?
Daniel and his lions
Surely, could do much worse;
If you take from others

Belongings not of you,
Just as it is given
Takes He the same from you;
But He loves the numbers
Like you, He takes good count
Calibrate the Son's days
Like Three Days on the Mount

Tempest snake is captured
My company she keeps
Level come the mountains
I topple them to sea
With your traps and snares,
I offer you cool drink
Pour the precious water
Fresh fountain of my sink
Take it past the doorway
After laid, the new floor
Hot, the sweaty Latin, drips from every pore
Accomplished is the conspiracy, as cool water concludes the
symbolic chore

Behold, but there is more!
Come inside Dead Devil

____ ____ ____ ____

Need I implore?
As helter skelter,
Seek ye not a shelter?
Seek ye not a Super Dome?
Seek ye not the dual birds' nest
To seat the birds your minions have flown?
High stairways so inviting,
'Tis Paradise you seek?
Just beyond the fiery doorways,
Stairs once ascended, in bodies, smoke, and dust descend
Murderers
Multiply their bounty of seventy two beautiful virgins
By the magnitude of their sin
Virgins promised to greet them at the height of your dead end

No Mas
Is to No Mass
Is to No Mosque
Is to No Mask
I say without a grin
Think me not a ____
As ___, I'm out to win!
Now, come the new owners
Crafty Cuban couple who hate ____
Although they eat for breakfast
Bowls of cereal and ____ droppings
Like plump raisins, they make a great ____
Now, come my old neighbors
In Greensburro, NC them I strangely see
Yet, they pay no notice, nor do they speak
Pretend not to see?
Why wonders me?
Now, even comes my one ____
As if from another mother
Abandon me does he
At Greedy Foison, they pretend not to see
Mysteries unfolding
At center I, the key
Do I see the future
As the past and present reveal to me
The home grown conspiracy
Dictate to the dark night
The day before I see?
How can that be, silly?

See blood moon on the rising,
See blood moon, the reddish glow,
See bloody orange carnage,
See how the harvest moon
Bleeds low
As it grows

Spanish cocker spaniels
Lap dogs of misery burn like the napalmed S A trees, weeds, and
coca leaves
Say you like that crack raw?

373

As I yearn the tempest snake
Have you the English lockjaw,
And like the snake, no hand to shake?
Who makes mountains stand
Or makes mountains erase?
We are not so grand
When families we obliterate

Troubled are The Four Horsemen
Their stable shall not keep
Sword in mouth White Rider
My, my, my Lord, your thigh wound is quite deep
No Mas
No Mass
No Mosque
No Mask
That hides the face
Know only constant conflict; know not peace?
Oh! You shall know His love and hate
You, who don't coincide,
You, who can't share a place on a pebble in space
You who don't coincide with WASPS
The cruel, ruling race

Yankee dollars only
The thing of copper cents
Keeps the "High and Mighty" down and lowly
Unless the oil is spent
Dare you block the Passage,
Israel is our "best" friend
WASPS will send you packing
And nuke you with a grin
As WASPS seek another,
Oil rich beneath the sand
Dare not touch Israel
Love for her is grand
Babylon is babble
As you may, think this verse
My words don't come lightly
Perhaps they veil an ominous curse,
The curse of worst as destiny's guarantee?

Respect not the Bible,
Pirates of land and sea?
Shall descend the Living Water;
Your ridge homes you'll never again see
As they are reclaimed
Proclaimed as God's alone
Just like I, as lone stranger, tried to make Grandnight Ridge my
new home
Take a chance,
Security and rent advanced,
To make a "fresh start", humble, Hypoint home?
Littered sewer swept before me,
I did bid you please to clean,
But you sent assassins
To crush the truth and dreams
Saw you not the future
Laid all through the vacant house?
Did you take the "personal", precious things
Including a pretty pictured frog and her gecko spouse?
Gecko's sell insurance
Yet, I can stake no claim
I made villain, victim, and trespasser
As three black White witches do make false claims
Told never to come back
So cold the trail of ice
When comes the new winter,
Well come sewer rats, mice, fleas, bedbugs, and lice

If new renters carry bedbugs,
Then appropriate the home,
Sacks of scum, the warlock White men and black White witches
Of Grandnight Ridge,
Should never sleep alone
Ridge, the home of mudslides
Don't listen as forewarned
Rain can come aplenty
Comes with the heavy storms
That's poetic justice
Penned for residential, rental creeps and freaks
Who "by law" stole and sold
My fine clothes, new furniture, new cars

And truck too!
Flat screens, computer, printer, and digital cameras
Are there no laws for you?
I have a solution,
God's justice is never late
You sit on a mountain ridge
Bid my Father to shake;
Make a platter of mud cakes
Or is it the mud pie
I have forgotten which?
If a warlock is the Demon's bitch
Then Grey Spectre's a phenomenal, financial
Trilateral trick

It's my losses
I aim to regain
By telling the truth
By ellipses or changing a name

Either way,
You know your guilt
Covers the infested bed where you lay
Like a patchwork quilt

Now, don't go and blame me,
Should houses sink and fall
I'm just a Simple Simon,
With words, houses don't fall

Take a little mixture
Of what I know to be,
Duck and run for cover,
Stand ground and let things be,

Hope the little children
Used the pool and learned to swim,
You'd take every life preserver
To save your lives of selfish sin

Rats, if need be, swim the deep;
Eels, if hungry enough, make them the treat
Vermin, carriers of more vermin,

With you they long too sleep

But
By the power
He
Has given me
Powerless
In every way
Shaped
In His very image
The living
Breathing clay

Comes the Living Water
To swim, to romp, to play
To drink, to bathe, to slay
To make the evil pay

Beneath the West over is the great geyser,
Yellowstone unawake, unshaken
The atomic clock's precise decimation most timely indeed
Synchronized should Donnie C's forsaken heart unnaturally stops
breaking

You laugh with wicked glee
Now, does come the question,
Did He repent in vain?
If God has already lost One Son,
I have lost two
While playing a foolish mind, body, and soul game

Now that you are happy
And sodomized the child;
Doubles are your pleasures
But troubled are your smiles
Coming to your senses,
Reality undone,
You have not seen Jesus
Unholy is the "First, Sixth Trumpet, One"
Count upon your fingers
The syllables of song

Triple check your answers' accuracy
Pray your calculations are not wrong
So six the sick can be!
When you only count them,
And yet, you fail to see!
Only "One" before you
"Triple Cross", "Trinity", "The True Three"
Math and your computers
Still hide the mystery
Simple Simon knows them
His name is Donnie C.
Silver tongue
Swift tricky
Streaks truth like lies mercury

Troubled are The Four Riders
Their stable shall not keep
Sword in mouth, Pale Rider
My, my, my Lord, your thigh wound is quite deep

Disbelief in God
Disregard for life
Your family, friends, and my foes
Will experience what it's like

To have one's honor trampled
To have one's ___ defiled
To hear the screams of torture
To see the contorted child

Kiss the lips as ass to mouth
The child whines, "What drink is this?"
"How foul the thing you ask,
You tell of me to kiss!"

Multiple is my pain
Please, multiply as due
The fire that shall rain
As the worst of hurricanes shall do

Bid as if at auction
It's a fire sale on young and old lives

Gaping holes in the Home and Flood Insurance,
Is it a sin to lie?

Yellowstone, the time bomb,
The lonely clock of tears
As was in my bedroom
Shadowy thorns around the grey, clock faced sphere

Did you care to notice, Grandnight
The bedroom DVD player's rare, hindquarter stock,
Rider in the dark place,
Entered without a knock,
Wasn't the footage, sadistically speaking, redneck poker hot?
Wasn't the "cum shot" absolutely infamous and defamed?
Bet you showed your male children
How to "cut" the best game?

Riders' commentary on cable
As painful as is seen
Graphic in its nature,
Shows the "art" of tortured scream

Proud as goats in Hades,
You advertise the graft,
Show the mechanism,
As if spine is not bone,
Sodomy,
As art,
Is craft

German Unit Master,
My loved one's never fixed?
"Wish" upon your "White" children,
"With all types of "White trash" and "nonwhite" blood they will
mix
Like an HIV, full blown AIDS, homosexual heroin fix"
Now, will you kill your offspring,
Nappy headed, mixed breed, bastard child?
You shall "never" love them?
Offspring will never smile?
They soon know that Daddy,

Donald T. Williams

The beast in darkened room,
Pulls back baby's covers
But only one is forever doomed

Deviate in nature
You'll ___ the half-breed child,
Drown them in the river quick,
Never face your denial,
And never face "man's" trial.

Pay or beg your redneck brother, the cop
Look the other way
Lawyers, Judges, CO's
Wear the steel tipped, white to red laced boot
Badges, guns, and vests guilt and bulletproof
Gutter secret society so high and aloof
Those who practice witchcraft,
Who say, "He's a Simple Simon no one",
Like gremlins on an aircraft,
Would undo Air Force One

God foreshadowed Negro, Nigger, Nigga
I, perhaps, could be
A "Gosh, who done it?" mystery
Who blocks the earth of Sun,
Who Martians love so dearly,
(And of this you would know,
If like me, you could see clearly)
Who, for red Moons, waits to come
As he waits for One to come, the Son

Love you
The Vampire and Wolfman flicks?
Your blood, your waste
Are His next date movie to rate for taste
Your flesh and bones
Are His to pick

Simple, Sorcerer Simon?
Your gist has gone too far;
As does twinkle afar
The North Star

Yellowstone, the time bomb sobs
As the axis tips and sways
Disarray most unnatural
As the balance of things misbehaves

Who can keep proper time?
Seasons are strangely changing
Animals are confused
Migration patterns are rearranging

Cracked is the looking class
For Death, there is no distinction
No longer the cares of class
All things living, face extinction

Now the end is coming,
Oh, calendar of Doom!
It was always coming
Whether or not
You read
The Bible,
A Mayan artifact,
Or Donnie C's poetic tunes

You "did" care to notice, Grandnight
The DVD's rare stock,
Rider in the dark place,
Redneck's poker hot
Knot as tight as my neck choker?
Bloody as the pen of Bram Stoker?

Cauldron, the graphite lead
Sharpened as a pencil
Graphite and wood wed
Not to skimp on details
I know how it matters does the size!
Graphite and "redwood" wed,
For you, the redneck, known for the rough ride
For you, the redneck bride,
For you, the hateful, redneck child,
For you, the wishful single breed, who scorns the weeds of wild
Can you trace your father?

Checked the woodpile each day?
Mandingoes, the great Black lovers
Had more than their share of plantation sex play
Could he be your grandfather? Great, Great, Great!
If so, you'd never say
Could Sadie be your grandmother? Great, Great, Great!
White Missy Master had her ways
Buck had to do "'xactly" what Missy Master say
Any given night, any given day
Washington had his share
How about Jefferson?
That_____ lover never cared
Now, you are all upset
Want to double and triple check
President Obama I bet

That's right
Call Him "Mr. President"
Politics, you must know, has its price
Protocol dictates it
Even if "you" don't like it one bit
Closed doors and mikes only know the names he's called
Flies upon the walls are appalled by the names
"Our President" is called
Spy flies by water coolers
Listen with intense ears
Big Brother is watching
Their plans our greatest fear

But
By the power
He
Has given me
Powerless
In every way
Shaped
In His very image,
The living,
Breathing clay

SO BLACK, SO BOLD, SO BEAUTIFUL: FM 88.8

By Donald T. Williams

Free Man 88.8
Williams can be so egotistical
Free Man 88.8
Thinks of self as mystical

Words rise from the hole
Atop the shoulders high
Prompted by long needle's
Inject to his left thigh

Right from the moment
Wakes he from lengthy sleep
Conquered is the mountain
Whose top he has now seen

Promised Land so tempting
Does not appear so far
No longer than the arms' length
Twinkles the farthest star

On the tip of fingertip
Shines brightly in the night
Place for me to call home
When the time is right

Inflate the man of solar winds
With God's speed, to earth he's bound
Mobile mammal moves miraculously
Parallel to the ground

Clipped winged cripple conquers
Chains crafted to confine

Darkness came before the dawn
After, the Son does shine

Die defeated shackles!
Hold not his body or his beautiful mind
Die defeated shackles!
Fly free his heart and "please" be kind

So shocked the insensitive system
That "specializes" in stifling strong spirited souls
Dumbfounded are the jailors
How could they lose their hold?

"Stiff"
The competition
In the battle of strong wills
Muscles
Don't mean anything
If thoughts "alone" commit the kill

Unfair, the advantage?
What does mankind know of "fair"?
When shoe is placed left right of wrong,
Suffer on or off as bare

Tell me
How it feels to be under control?
If I spin my wheels,
Then "Take Off" is a Go!

Ducks can waddle or fly
Depending on their mood
Ducks can swim or dive
Either is what they do

Some birds eat only the living
Some birds eat only the dead
Some words can be kind or unkind
Better off said or left unsaid?

Free Man 88.8
Williams can be so egotistical

Free Man 88.8
Thinks of self as mystical
Birds of prey may think
They rule the skies alone
They may even eat alive or dead flesh,
Drink blood and suck the marrow of bone

But the birds who pray
As I say and believe, "By God, they do!"
Have a distinctive, instinctive, believer's advantage
Over those who don't or care not to

Weird words, wise of unwise
Rise from the high, shouldered hole
Laughing gas and helium premium blend
Does good to lift, heart, mind, and soul

Adding to the benefit
Is when feet take to air
There may be some wings afoot
Can you not see them there?

Confined imaginations,
Like imprisoned bodies, hearts, and minds,
See no silver linings or rainbows,
Understand no reason or rhyme

Free Man 88.8
As egotistical as he can be
Writes with reason, rhyme, rhythm, and rainbows
As are the ways of poetry

Shoot down as is your custom
Shoot down as is your sport
Your conceit does have a formidable rival
Not to mention a profound contempt of court

See I do the exorcist's turned head
The old, so called "wise" White owl so high sat
Eyes, a dead yellow wide
Belly full of snakes and rats

Try burst the inflated ego
Try prick the conceited bag of wind
In a fight with my righteous indignation
'Tis certain;
Your evil can not win

Free Man 88.8
Williams can be so egotistical
Free Man 88.8
Thinks of self as mystical

Free Man 88.8
As egotistical as he can be
Writes with reason, rhyme, rhythm, and rainbows
As are the ways of poetry

Across
The earthly airwave's span
Across
The Universe "Oh, so grand!"
Transmissions sent
As well received
Only fools,
Fail to believe

Never over
Never out
So eternal
Know thy clout

Martin Luther King Jr.
I may not be
But who's to say
The "King of Kings" hasn't "sanction" me

Backdoor deals and kickbacks
Give Unions a black eye
Scandals and corruption are prevalent
That's no fiction or lie

Pride and conceit
May be a sin

But who's to say
Donnie C won't be forgiven?

Religious zealots
Without an ounce of Christ
Will say, "Hell no!"
And pray that they're right

Like any protégé
An intern or apprentice must put in work
And remember
I was a teacher, bank, and a postal clerk

Proud in my Association
Proud of my Affiliation
Payer of Union dues
'Twas the path I chose

Love I,
My comrade pushers of paper
Love I,
The productive pupil maker, pusher, and shaper

No.
I'm not a Socialist
Capitalism has, can, and will continue to work,
But
Only if the business playing field is leveled fair;
Racism like ours is still an obstacle;
Obliterate and clear the air

I spies
All around us,
But the blind eye does betray
As
It looks the other way
Yet, honest, hardworking people should trust you
People of and with potential but not born yesterday

Just like the "lucky baby boomer"
Hands get dirty and boots love the dirt
Can't you think tank, smartest guys in the room

Donald T. Williams

Stop jerking off on one another and finally get down to work?

Yes, I speak most frankly
When my family, wife, mind, ego, and libido
You attempt to murder, crush, or abuse
Cannons and missiles are for firing, and man, I love to cruise

Spies all around US
Crucial secrets bought and sold
As your greatest resource, our people
Grow up dumb, obese, inert, brain dead, addicted, immoral, and
emotionally cold

God Bless America
As if you "really" give a damn
If those words were ever true,
You'd put "poor people"
First
Not the "rich man"

Sell your people out
Likewise,
You sell out yourselves
China, debt, and oil will make a slave of US all
Serve "you, America's rich few" a taste of poverty's Hell

Slavery is an experience
Soon enough you'll know
Can't you feel your shackles
Sure as the "Bag of Wind" does blow?

Free Man 88.8
Williams can be "so" egotistical
Free Man 88.8
Thinks "conceitedly of self" as mystical

Free Man 88.8
As "self important" and boastful as he can be
Writes with reason, rhyme, rhythm, and rainbow
As are the ways of poetry

Inflate the man of solar winds
With God's speed, to earth he's bound
Mobile mammal moves miraculously
Parallel to the ground

Across
The earthly airwave's span,
Across
The Universe "Oh, so grand!"
Transmissions sent
As well received
Only fools,
Fail to believe

So Black
So Bold
So Beautiful
Free Man 88.8

Best for "you" to appease
For none can close the open Horsemen's Gate
Pray that mercy
Wins over hate,
But
Know in your black hearts
Prayers are now too late

The long, hard ride
Will not make
Either
Rider
Or
Horse
Thirst
Or
Break
Both
Rider
And
Horse
Know well what it takes

To make man and man's world
Tremble in their wake

Pricked the purple bubble,
Bubble so sublime
So personal and impersonal
Was your crime

Now
Victorious
Vengeance
I pray you find
My Father's
More hideous than mine

Free Man 88.8
Williams can be so egotistical
Free Man 88.8
Thinks of self as mystical

"Stiff"
The competition
In the battle of strong wills
Muscles
Don't mean anything
If thoughts "alone" commit the kill

Never over
Never out
Never doubt
Thy Father's Clout

DONNIE C's CREW

By Donald T. Williams

There have been several Black men
Who have had an influence on Donnie C

First there is my father
The head of my first family

He was an interstate truck driver
Before that an Army man serving his country

Loving husband and dad,
He taught me how to walk tall, love, and handle adversity

Poker player and gambling great
Quick to anger and retaliate

My dad was always clean as a tack
My father was a no bullshit cat

Always looked up to him
Held him to a very high degree

Seems a lot of my father
Surges through the veins in me

"Bitch ain't been born who can take my money"
And with him I totally agree

This conviction and others are in my genes
A genetic part of my family tree

Other influential Black men
Were TV and big screen heroes alike

Book smart, streetwise, and slick

Rough and tumble role models with bite and kick

Bigger than life
As bold as any Black boy could hope to be

I'm talking
Cassius Clay aka Mohammed Ali

I'm talking
John Shaft aka Richard Roundtree
Jim Brown

Mr. T

All the Sugar Rays

Ice Cube and Ice T

I'm talking
Sweet Back, Melvin Van Peebles and Mario Van Peebles

Redd Foxx and Desmond Wilson

Trouble Man, Robert Hooks and Kevin Hooks

Curtis Mayfield

Seal

Tyrese

Eddie Kendricks

David Ruffin

Sidney Poitier

Don Cornelius (My Soul Train)

Antonio Fargas (My "No Restrictions" Man)

The Mack

Master P

Leon

Mike Tyson

Lynn Swan

Isley Brothers (Ron, My Mr. Big)

Isaac Hayes

Billy D Williams

Marvin Gaye

Dominique Wilkens

Isaac Hayes

Clevon Little (My Blazing Saddles)

Jack Johnson (My Ultimate Pugilist)

Barry White

Robert Townsend (My Hollywood Shuffle)

Dion Sanders (My Prime Time Man)

Wayans Brothers

O.J. Simpson

Johnnie L. Cochran Jr.

Smokey Robinson

Sean Combs

Michael Jordan

Will Smith (My Fresh Prince, My Bad Boy, and My Legend Man)

Bill Russell (My Boston Celtic)

Charlie Russell

Grant Hill!

Biggy Smalls (My Do or Die Bed Stuy Big Pappa)

Jimi Hendrix (My Voodoo Child)

Michael Jackson (My King of Pop)

Barry Gordy

George Gervin (My Ice Man, Pharaoh of the Finger Roll)

Dr. J. (My Sky Walker)

And, of course, Jay Z (My Do and Thrive Bed Stuy Guy)

Harry Belafonte (My Day-O!)

Nick Van Exel (My Rock Handler Man)

Fifty Cents (My Hood Survivor Man)

James Earl Jones (My "One of a Kind" Man)

Spud Webb (My Higher Heights Man)

Rapper's Delight

Barry Sanders

Public Enemy (Flavor Flav, What time is it?)

Clarence Clemons (My East Street Band Man)

Adam Clayton, Jr. (My King of Harlem)

Pigmeat Markham (My "Here Comes the Judge" Man)

Ike Turner

Ray Nagin

R. Kelly (My "I Believe I Can Piss on You" Man)

Forrest Whitaker (My Ghost Dog)

Fred Williamson (My Hammer)

Wyclef Jean (My Fugee)

Terrance Howard (My Thespian and Math Teacher)

RuPaul (My Sista Man)

Stokely Carmichael

Jefferson Thomas (My Civil Right Pioneer)

Roscoe Lee Brown (My Man of Distinction)

Ray Charles

Bishop Milton Hines-Dortch (Mount Calvary Baptist Church; Bkly, NY 11233)

Denzel Washington (My Training Day Nigga)

Percy Sutton

Michael Wright (My Sugar Hill Man)

Richard Pryor (My Ground Breaking Comedian)

Hill Harper (My Lackawanna Blues Man)

H. Rap Brown

Mean Joe Green

Moses Gunn (My Original Gangster)

Martin Luther King, Jr.

Huey P. Newton (My Black Panther Man)

Judge Joe Brown (My Black Chief Justice of Court TV)

Adrian Fenty

Jerome Bettis (My Steelers' Big Bad Bus)

Nelson Mandela (My Red, Black, and Green Man)

Muggsy Bogues

Sammy Davis, Jr. (My Mr. Bojangles, My Candyman and Rat Packer)

Smoking Joe Frazier

Ron Moody (My Nigger's Nigga)

Bob Marley (My Rasta Man)

Carl Johnson (My Principal, CSD 16, Bklyn, NY)

Mercury Morris

Paul Winfield

James Ingram

Bill Cosby (My Eye Spy, and Dr. Heathcliff Huxtable)

Johnnie Taylor

Malcolm-Jamal Warner (My Theo Huxtable)

Doug Wilder (My Virginian)

Martin Lawrence (My Bad Boy and Big Mamma)

Sinbad

DMX

Bernie Mac

Gale Sayers

Bobby Blue Bland (My Blues)

Zephriam Cummings (My Principal, CSD 16, Bklyn, NY)

Run D-MC

Carl Weathers (My Action Jackson)

Spinners

Temptations

Smokey Robinson (and My Miracles)

Stevie Wonder

Keith Sweat

Eddie "Rochester" Anderson

Bill Bellamy

Marion Barry (My Political Piper)

James Almos (My Good Times)

Bobby Womack

Nick Cannon

DJ Jazzy Jeff

Rev. Al Sharpton

Frank Mickens (My Principal, CSD 16, Bklyn, NY)

Jessie Jackson

Jessie Jackson Jr. (My Congressman)

Alfonso Ribeiro (My Carlton Banks)

James Avery (My Judge Zeke Philip Banks)

Oscar Polk (Fleetfoot, My Cabin in the Sky Man)

Jerry Rice (My "Sure Hands" Man)

Paul Robeson

Reggie White (My Defensive End and Minister)

Walter Payton (My Sweetness)

George Clinton (My P Funk All Stars)

Bill Dukes (My Thespian and Director)

Robert Norris (My Principal, CSD 16, Bklyn, NY)

John Hope Franklin (My Scholar)

Nelly ("It's I Hot in Here", Man)

Bootsy Collins

John Coltrane

Kenneth Edmonds (My Babyface)

Dizzy Gillespie

Louis Armstrong

Cab Calloway (My hi-de-hi)

Buster Douglas

Duke Ellington (My A Train)

Count Basie

Bobby Short

Miles Davis

Ron Ivey (My Supervisor, CSD 16, Bklyn, NY)

The Delfonics

Cuba Gooding, Sr.

Cuba Gooding, Jr.

Morris Chestnut

Taye Diggs

Wesley Snipes (My "Action Hero")

Grover Washington, Jr.

Lou Rawls (My "You'll Never Find" Man)

The Chi Lites

Carl Lewis

World B. Free (My E.N.Y "NBA Real Deal")

John Singleton

The Hudlin Brothers (My Movie Directors)

Busta Rhymes

Sherman Hemsley (Mr. George Jefferson)

Marvin Hagler

Mos Def

Frankie Lymon

Steve Harvey

Tom Joyner

Sly Stone (and My Family Stone)

Luther Vandross

Don Cheadle

Otis Redding

Gamble and Huff

The Brothers Johnson

Melvin Ottey (My A.I.D.P Man, CSD 16, Bklyn, NY)

Teddy Pendergrass

Tupac Shakur

Frankie Crocker (My WOR "Love Man")

Kobe Bryant

Petey Greene

James Brown (My Godfather of Soul)

Tiger Woods

George Johnson (My Afro Sheen)

Gregory Hines

Paul Williams

Parliament Funkadelic

Billy Paul

The O'Jays (My "Love Train" Men)

Earth, Wind and Fire

Lebron James

Al Vann (My District 36 Councilmen, Democrat)

Tommy Hearns (My Hitman)

Dr. Dre

Frank Lucas (My American Gangster)

Riddick Bowe

Hank Aaron

LL Cool J

Nelson Narcisse (Deacon, Mount Calvary Baptist Church, Bklyn, NY)

Ludacris

Frederick Douglas

Cool Mo De

Alexander O'Neil (My Fake, My Sunshine Man)

Eddie Griffin (My Voodoo Child Too!)

Lawrence Fishburn (My Cornbread, Earl and Me)

Lou Campanella

Macfadden and Whitehead

Allen Iverson (My Answer)

Ron O'Neal (My Super Fly)

Shemar Moore

Peabo Bryson (My Stop the Rain Man)

Arthur Ashe (My Tennis Man)

George Foreman (My Champion Grill Master)

Jason Kidd

Sugar Hill Gang

Walt "Clyde" Frazier

Leroy Jones (aka Amir Baraka, Civil Activist/Educator)

David Dinkins (My NYC Mayor)

Tony Todd (My Candy Man and Megatron)

Basil Patterson

The Whispers

Grandmaster Flash and The Furious Five (My Message)

David Patterson (My Governor of NYS)

John Stockton (My New York Knick)

Ed Lover and Dr. Dre

Snoop Dogg (My Gin and Juice)

Alex Haley (My Roots)

Lavar Burton (My Kute Kente)

Easy E

Robert Guillaume

William Marshall (My Shakespearian Actor and My "Blackula")

Joe Louis (My Brown Bomber)

Fab 5 Freddie

Eddie Murphy

Samuel L. Jackson

Sam Greenlee (My Spook Who Sat By The Door)

Calvin Lockhart (My King Willie, Predator 2)

Lawrence Hilton-Jacobs

Danny Glover

Thalmus Rasulala (My Cool Breeze)

Thurgood Marshal (My NAACP Lawyer, 1st Black Supreme Court Justice, and Roe vs Wade Segregation Man)

Spike Lee

Rick James (My Super Freak Man)

Bobby Brown (My Prerogative Man)

Tavis Smiley

John Johnson (My Mr. Ebony)

Joe Jackson (and My Jackson Five)

Flip Wilson

Colonel Abrahams (The Truth)

Dolemite

Julian Bond

Andrew Young

Clarence Thomas (My Supreme Court Justice)

Jackie Robinson

B.B. King (My Thrill is Gone)

Reggie Jackson (My Mr. October)

Morgan Freeman

Earl Monroe (My Pearl)

Charles Rangel (My US Rep. D. NY)

Clyde Drexel (My Glide)

Charles Barkley (My Round Mound)

The Four Tops

MC Hammer (My Hammer Time)

Jimmy Walker (My Dy-no-mite!)

Bo Diddley

Chris Brown (My Young Blood)

Darryl Dawkins (My Chocolate Thunder)

Tyler Perry (My "Medea" Man)

Arsenio Hall (My Late Night T.V Man, Woof, Woof!)

Richard Wright (My Black Boy, and Native Son Man)

Vaughn Harper (My WBLS "Quiet Storm")

Billy Preston

LT. Gen. Russell Honore' Ret. (My Katrina Man)

Prince (My "Purple Rain")

Ed Bradley (My "60 Minutes")

Amos and Andy (My Cab Driver Comedians)

King Fish (My Barber and Street Hustler)

Stymie (My "Little Rascal")

Buckwheat (My "Little Rascal" Too)

John Johnson (My ABC News Anchor Man)

TD Jakes (My Preacher Man)

Kirk Franklin (My Gospel Choir Man)

The Sensational Nighting Gales (My Heavenly Voices)

David Robinson (My Admiral)

Leroi Bennett (My Historian)

Dwayne Wade (My Miami Heat)

Randel Robinson (My Pan American Affairs Man)

Mr. Marsalis (My Musicians Father and Sons, Bradford and Winston)

Dave Chappel (My Nigga's Nigga)

Charlie Murphy (My Nigga's Nigga Too)

Naughty by Nature (My Treach)

Bow Wow (My Young Pitbull)

All of these Great Brothers have had an

Influence

A Positive Affect

And Effect

On Donnie C

All Of Them Are Great Black Men

No Matter Their

Glorious

Or Checkered History

Rev. Jerimiah Wright (My "God Damn American" Man)

Gerald Levert

Doc Rivers (My Celtic Coach)

Ray Allen (My Celtic)

Magic Johnson

Paul Pierce (My Celtic)

Kevin Garnett (My Celtic)

Alonso Mourning

Karl Malone (My Mailman)

Connie Hawkins

Kareem Adul-Jabar

Wilt Chamberlin (My Stilt)

Meadow Lark Lemon (My Harlem Globe Trotter)

Curley (My Harlem Globe Trotter Man Too!)

Avery Johnson

Nate Archibald

Michal Steele (My Republican?)

Steve Harvey

Michael Dorn (My Worf, Star Trekker)

Reggie Miller (My "Sure Shot" Pacer)

D.L. Hughley

Tyson Beckford (My Super Male Model)

Tony Dungy (My Super Bowler)

Cedric (My Entertainer)

Emmet Smith (My Cowboy)

Lenny Wilkins

Michael Irvin (My "All Hands" Cowboy Too!)

Jackie Wilson

Scottie Pippen

Rev. Herbert Daughtry (Pastor, House of the Lord Church, Brooklyn, N.Y.)

C.L. Franklin

James Cleveland

Boyz 2 Men

Little Anthony and My Imperials

Russell Simmons

Joe Dumars

Louis Gossett Jr.

2 Live Crew

Al Greene

Tuskegee Airmen

James Worthy

Glenn Thurman

Evander Holyfield

Blair Underwood

The Flamingoes

Delroy Lindo

Buster Douglas

Avery Johnson

Keith David

Rocky Carroll

Elijah Muhammad

AC Greene

Shaquille O'Neal

Brian McKnight

Dave Bing

The Pips

New Edition

Louis Farakhan

Patrick Ewing

Kaseem Hardison

Tony Dorsett

John Thompson

A.Phillip Randolf

Woody Strode (My Black Cowboy)

Huge Masakela

Charles S. Dutton

Dave Winfield

Chauncey Billups

Jayson Williams (My Tough Luck Baller)

Michael Johnson (My Gold Shoes Man)

Craig Morris (My Mission Impossible Man)

Ving Rhames (My Mission Impossible Man Too)

Lionel Richie

Ernie Hudson (My Ghostbuster)

Desmond Tutu

David Allen Grier

Mekhi Phifer

Larenz Tate

Al Roker (My Weatherman)

Neil DeGrasse Tyson (My Director, Hayden Planitarium)

Garret Morris (My Saturday Night Live Man)

Jamie Foxx

Darryl Strawberry

Jesse Owens (My Original Olympics Man)

Chris Rock

Brock Peters

Curtis Blow

Roland Martin (My CNN Man)

Kanye West

Stephen A. Smith (My Radio/Talk Show Host)

Shaka Zulu

Kweisi Mfume (My U.S. Rep. and Pres. NAACP)

Richard Bratton (English Teacher, Retired, Thomas Jefferson H.S.
Bklyn, NY)

Ken Norton (My Mandingo Champion)

Owen Thompson (My A.I.D.P Man, CSD 16, Bklyn, NY)

Khalid Abdul Muhammad (My Nation of Islam and New Black
Panther Party Man)

Henry Louis Gates Jr. (My Faces of America Man)

Bokeem Woodbine (My Gifted Thespian)
Donald Adeosun Faison

Barack Obama (President of the USA)

The more Donnie C. reflects,
The more his crew list gets longer and longer.

The more Donnie C. recalls,
His respect and homage gets stronger and stronger
These mighty Black men were
And still are my brotherly heroes
Fantastic male human specimens
Whose colors are jet black
Dark chocolate, milk chocolate
Rich mocha, tan or simply some shade
Of ebony brown

Just color them "human" and worthy of a regal crown

Donald T. Williams

All of these great brothers
Have had an influence,

A positive affect
On Donnie C

All of them are Great Black Men
No matter their glorious or checkered
History.

PART NINE
OLIVE BRANCH

I AM UPSET

By Donald T. Williams

I am upset
But I don't hate
I fish for men
My poems as bait

The lines I cast
Work as a net
The more I cast
The more men I get

Catch and return
I do of some
They spread the word
The Holy Spirit has chosen some

To spread the peace
And/or spread the grief
All this depends
On man's belief or disbelief

Belief in God
Or in man's world
Which of the two
Is the true pearl?

My Father plays
With marbles round
The universes
Are His playgrounds

His marbles spin
Ejected from finger and thumb
They clash and smash
His amusement and fun

Stars self implode
As a cycle of life
Black Holes given birth
Magnets of energy and light

Do they cast lines
As if to fish?
Starfish are real
As is a wish?

I am upset
But I don't hate
I fish for men
My poems as bait

The lines I cast
Work as a net
The more I cast
The more men I get

Catch and return
Is a humanely kind thing
And I do hope
Bigger catches practice brings

But like any man
I have to eat
Some fish of the sea
Are like a meat

Fresh fish food
Need not be
The chicken
Of the sea

Fresh fish food
Could very well be
The souls of men
Caught and set free by God's mercy

I am upset,
But I don't hate
I fish for men
My poems are bait

The lines I cast
Work as a net
The more I cast
The more men I get

Catch and return
I do of some
They spread the word
The Holy Spirit has chosen some

To spread the peace
And/or spread the grief
All this depends
On Man's belief and disbelief

Belief in God
Or in Man's world
Which of the two
For you, is the true pearl?

I am upset
But I can love
Forgive but never forget
How my honor was assaulted
How my pride was mauled

My Father plays
With marbles round
The universes
Are His playgrounds

His marbles spin
Ejected from fingers and thumbs
As earthly spiders spin works of art
Sticky web works as traps for more than one

Donald T. Williams

Deadly Black Widow weaves webs
Same as nets
That fish for flies
And get great gnats

I am upset,
But I can love
As did and does the Son
Still casts nets of love

LIES IN THE NIGHT A RING OF TRUTH

By Donald T. Williams

Confess what ye did
That ye may live
Lies in the night
The truth in light

Moonbeams and stars
Light from afar
Travel on their own
To here be shone

As does the sun,
The distant one
Give solar care
The planets share

What's done in dark
Comes out in light
Nothing is hidden
From the Father's sight

What you could tell
He does well know
Each and every bell
Is His to toll

A ring of truth
His ear to hear
Will make it bright,
Your darkest fear

Such full relief
Comes with the day,
But first the night
Moves out of way

Confess what ye did
That ye may live
Lies in the night
The truth in light

Evil schemes are prison bars
Like white feathers stuck to tar
Exposed, displayed for all to see
Coming clean great task indeed

True, the truth shall set you free
True, this is as it should be
Lay down your blight, your misery
In light, plain sight for all to see

Moonbeams and stars
Light from afar
Travel on their own
To be here shone

Such full relief
Comes with the day,
But first the night
Moves out of way

What's done in dark
Comes out in light
Nothing is hidden
From the Father's sight

What you could tell
He does well know
Each and every bell
Is His to toll

A ring of truth
His ear to hear
Will make it bright,
Your darkest fear

Such full relief
Comes with the day,
But first the night
Moves out of way

Confess what ye did
That ye may live
Lies in the night
The truth in light

As dark tree bark
Covers light wood rings
Beneath the bark
Rings tell of things

Within you,
True things reside
Just beneath,
Your lying hide

Cut to truth
Extract without pride
Better out than in
The splinters of lies

Such full relief
Comes with the day,
But first the night
Moves out of way

Confess what ye did
That ye may live
Lies in the night
The truth in light

Within you,
True things reside
Just beneath,
Your lying hide

A ring of truth
His ear to hear
Will make it bright,
Your darkest fear

SPINNING WHEEL

By Donald T. Williams

You won't answer questions, Babe
Do you know I speak the truth?
Lies reek like a cancer, Babe
Unpleasantness permeates from floor to roof

Live indeed in the home that "we" built
Keep all the capital gains from "our" first
Lie to me about everything, Babe
And still keep secrets that are worst

Life's a spinning wheel, Babe
Brass rings just out of reach
Folks like spokes go round and round
As tides come and go on the beach

When love becomes expendable and broken hearts unmendable,
When _____ are caught, gutted, and released,
____ may no longer be defendable
When their offenses would give Satan grief

Pretentiousness is your stately grace
You remain distant and aloof
Not look me in the eyes
Not even when face to face

Such are the nuances
Which give you away
Guilt can be a trip
And you're on excursions every day

Life's a spinning wheel, Babe
Brass rings just out of reach
Folks like spokes go round and round
As tides come and go on the beach

Love "is not" expendable
Even when malicious acts are reprehensible
No man or woman is invincible,
But some once foolish folks can become quite sensible

You won't answer questions, Babe
No matter how much I beseech,
Yet my prayers have been answered, Babe
Through my poetry, I still teach

The world is now my cracked oyster
A four walled _____ and classroom were once my shell
The Grey Spectre has returned to free me from my demons
Said, "Donnie, My Boy, if need be, give 'em hell!"

Miraculous metamorphism via a bowl of sacred mushroom soup?
Kafka thought he was a cockroach
I've a rapport with a Grey Spectre "head" coach
Whose smile I've never seen droop

Miraculous metamorphism as in a butterfly's first flight
As his new self is born again from his old self's caterpillar cocoon
This can only be God's love,
And I can't help but swoon

True, you called me "crazy"
Even so, in my eyes and ears you looked and sounded so "damn"
cute
Love so blind, it took some time to realize
Your big feet were about to give me the boot

Pretentiousness is your stately grace
You remain distant and aloof
Not look me in the eyes
Not even when face to face

You won't answer questions, Babe
Do you know I speak the truth?
Lies reek like a cancer, Babe
Unpleasantness permeates from floor to roof

Lie to me about everything
Keep secrets that are worst
Long, tall, feminine drink of cool water,
Would you have me die of thirst?

Life's a spinning wheel, Babe
People you love just out of reach
Folks like spokes go round and round
As tides come and go like strangers on the beach

LOVE'S FRUIT

By Donald T. Williams

Fresh as fish on Friday
Or a lobster caught off Maine
Thoughts of you come to me
Sure as spring does bring the rain

Wonder how you're doing?
Wonder how your look has changed?
Wonder if you still love me?
Wonder if still burns the flame?

Though my needs are simple
There still lives a need for you
In between my temples
Live the thoughts of love so true

I am not sadistic
Taking pleasure in no pain
Are you a statistic?
Just a number without name?

How many have fallen
To the ways of world and sin!
There is chance for changing
If you want it deep within

Accept my invitation
To some dinner on a date
My love's fresh as ever
You, indeed, may fill your plate

Fresh as fish on Friday
Or a lobster caught off Maine
Thoughts of you come to me
Sure as spring does bring the rain

Wonder how you're sleeping?
Wonder if my face appears?
Wonder if your rollovers
Still embrace me not there?

Many are the nights I've spent
You imagined by my side
Honeymoon-lit nuptials
Of a love knot loose yet tied

Heartstrings once drawn together
Love's abstinence need no longer exist
Confront without anger
Let our lips bare blissful kiss

Fresh as figs in springtime
On a lush Mediterranean tree
May our love grow bountiful
Be the fruit on which we feed

Though my needs are simple
There still lives a need for you
In between my temples
Live the thoughts of love so true

Foolish, wishful thinking?
Never, when the heart speaks truth
Finally breaking bread with you
Will be the living proof

Fresh as fish on Friday
Or a lobster caught off Maine
Thoughts of you come to me
Sure a spring does bring the rain

Fresh as figs in springtime
On a lush Mediterranean tree
May our love grow bountiful
Be the fruit on which we feed

DREAMS

By Donald T. Williams

Seems as if the word is out
Sisters leave that man alone
You see that man's heart is spoken for
He just appears to be on his own

Brother's life is tied up
In a love his heart can't shake
Brother's love is held captive
In dreams from which he can't wake

Dreams of a college sweetheart
Dreams of thirty-plus years in a knot
Dreams of a true love once tender
That now stinks of shit and rot

Happily ever after
Was not the script for me
Strangers stole and spoiled
The pudding cake
Of my sweet ____ love recipe

Perhaps they did not steal it
Perhaps she gave her love away
A woman scorned will bear her horns
With a Devil's shame and vanity

Day came I found her pot much bigger
It no longer suited me to a "T"
Now, there was no bottom
Where a bottom used to be

Wider than the Lincoln
Strangers drove and rammed her clear through
Now my_____a toll booth
And not the love I once knew

Now, she's known as _____
Equitable distribution has run its course
Now, I am left with next to nothing
Not even a "clean-break" _____

Seems I'm still a "fair catch"
Worth too much to completely throw away
More than "good for nothing"
Like every dog, I'll have my day

Now she's known as _____,
Yet for her I have no hate
She'll get all she has coming
Served cold on a Judgment Day hotplate

Seems as if the is word's out
Sisters, leave that brother alone
You see, that man is spoken for
He just appears to be alone

Brother's life is tied up
In a love his heart can't shake
Brother's love is held captive
In dreams from which he can't wake

I love her
What more can I say?
I love her,
But we've gone our own ways

Misery's not my company
This lone wolf does well alone
This may be my nature
But man's not meant to live alone

Step to me young lady
Recognize when I step to you
Step with me young lady
We can share our lives as two

Step to me young lady
Recognize when I step to you
Feel my flames without shame
Keep it real without games
Perhaps we'll find love
That is true

I loved her
What more can I say?
I'll love you!
Now let's share our blessed days

I'M WAITING

By Donald T. Williams

Maybe I should write
A full length book
Tell the world
How my world was shook

Get the entire weight
Of this bullshit off my chest
Cause and effect
Speak of regret

Find a nice, lovely woman
Who will
Love me
Fuck me
Suck me
Love me

Love me
Fuck me
Suck me
Love me
To help put all this heavy
Bullshit to final full rest

I'm getting older
High time I get back in the game
Take my shot,
Get on the boards, and claim my fame

God made plenty
Of good women worldwide
Surely, there is a "right" one
To stand with me at my side

Actually, I'm not "really" looking
I'm expecting to be found
Right-side up lucky Lincoln
Shining on USA ground

Someone will love and respect me
For who and what I am
Never take from me, never forsake me
Or make me feel like I'm less than a man

In return, I will love and adore
Respect her space and dependent, independency
Cherish our love as it grows
From infancy to ageless maturity

There'll be no physical,
Mental,
Or emotionally
Abusive, leashes, bounds, or chains

Tethered
To a spirit free
As it should be
Without fear of me

The lamp of knowledge
Burns its flame
Unrestrained
For her and me to gain

I will not
"take" her
"rape" her
"break" her

Like some fine filly __ fucked
Like some wildly domesticated lap dog
Who, while _____ my name, brought me shame
In each lurid Triple X DVD frame

Not even if she wants that

For it is true
That snakes eat rats
As it is true
Of pussy cats

On what you feast
Comes out your end
And chances are
You'll feast again

There just may be
An endless time
Eternity
Could be a grind

For those who snapped
The "whip" of love
Receive the same
From God above

Yesterday's sub-human hog
Same as today's Alpha Dog
Here to do the Devil's work
Defile all women in pants or skirt

Make them slaves
To their every whim
Nothing more
Than a piece of trim

Private toilet
Close at hand
Bidding done
Upon command

I desire
None of this
If I could,
I'd grant this wish

Donald T. Williams

None as sex slave
Gone Geisha Girl
Set them free
Throughout the world

Pimps no longer
Rule the roost
Break the chains
Of physical abuse

Long gone
Are the rites of rape,
Kidnappings
And the street life's fate

A woman is human
An essential part of me
With a right to freedom, choice,
And dignity

A counterpart
Subservient to me?
Only
If done willingly

Mutual love
Respect
Caring
Concern
Comfort
And regard

Are more like my cup
Of water
Milk
Juice
Soda
Beer
Wine
Liquor
Coffee
Or tea

Home girl, are you out there?
Donnie C's waiting for you to come home
And once you get here,
Don't switch up and roam

It's your choice
But please be sure
Donnie C won't tolerate
A lying, cheating whore

Hope has me inspired
Yet frankly, I'm really tired
Of the many nights alone
And waking up on the bone

And mind you,
Bones are good
I'm thankful
For the wood

I do encourage you
To hurry up some
I'd love to see your face, tits, and ass
Before my days are done

Good things come
To those who wait
I've learned patience,
But you're "good and late"

May sound selfish
Childish at best,
But I'll cry like a baby
Until some milk I get

This pot's boiling
There's a bubbling stew
Time's come for serving,
And it's long overdue

Get a move on
Get a groove on
Make yourself known
If you're street legal and grown

Too shy to step forward,
Afraid you too, may get dissed and dismissed,
Like some ____, ____, hooker, whoring school Principal
With a marital rift
And set adrift?

Be at ease
Don't tease
Donnie C's going to hold his cards
Very close to his chest and bulletproof vest

Pot shots at the heart
Better not start
Wigs will split
Skulls will part

Come with your best
Don't make a mess
Pass the "crack head" teacher's
Pop quizzes and final test

I'm waiting
Do your best!
But if my wish doesn't comes true,
It's for the best

COME VENUS

By Donald T. Williams

Come my way, Venus
Descend from the air
Goddess of beauty
Someone needs your care

Mend my broken heart
Cupid's arrow has been torn away
I've fallen all apart
Fading more with each day

Nights alone have rendered
A love that I held dear
To a ghostly figure
In dreams I've come to fear

Fear that will not come the day
When two reconcile
Let there be the words of truth
That no man is an isle

Where are the ladies
If I have no___?
Seems she's moved on down the road
Let's get on with life

Where are the ladies?
I could use some spice
Where are the ladies?
Some sugar would be nice

Come my way, Venus
Intervene in my affairs
Smile for me Venus
Play the vixen with your flair

Mend my broken heart
With a dose of good love today
Have Cupid take another shot at me
I make a handsome prey

Nothing like some good old "new" loving
To strike the match and bring forth passion's heat
Bring two hearts together
And match them beat for beat

Where are the ladies?
Who can sweeten a good man's life?
Where are the ladies?
Pure sugar with a dash of spice

Come my way, Venus
Descend from the air
Goddess of beauty
Someone needs your care

BUXOM BLACK BEAUTY

By Donald T. Williams

Aesthetic faculties
On sudden overdrive and overload
Absolutely astounded
By what my olfactory nerves and optics behold

Buxom Black Beauty
Heaven only could have sent
Wide eyes open
Flared nostrils greet her scent

Sober, awake yet dreaming
Better shut the door on my heart
Slow motion is dream weaving
This tapestry's end may be its start

Buxom Black Beauty
Heaven only could have sent
Better shut my gaping mouth
Too late, through it my heart just went

Physical, emotional overdrive and overload
How does an experienced man
Slip, trip, dip, and flip
For a woman, he doesn't even know?

Life as I know it
Can throw you some good and evil curves
Familiar and/or unknown roads can be treacherous
Dry or wet roads can make the experienced, safe driver swerve

Making first expressions
May be a clever or an awkward pass or fail test
Making first impressions
May be forgettable or memorable at best

Why pick one?
Why pass on all the rest?
Monogamy is a Biblical wish or myth?
Physical attraction and chemistry are science, not some restrictive
religious mess

Set self up for failure
If you think you've found the "one"
Chances are "someone" will creep
Vows are heavy words too hefty for hollow people to keep

If it's all about procreation,
Casual sex reveals a human flaw
Preserving pearls for a better world
Requires prerequisites before the thaw

Love at first sight?
Man, how silly can you be? Psych!
Quick chemical exchange, pumps the heart, rocks the brain?
Man, eyes play tricks and pheromones can smell so strange

No words need be spoken?
Man, you must be joking!
Preconceived and prearranged?
Man, the sounds buck wild and completely deranged!

Aesthetic faculties
On sudden overdrive and overload
Absolutely astounded
By what my olfactory nerves and optics behold

Buxom Black Beauty
Heaven only could have sent
Wide eyes open
Flared nostrils greet her scent

Better unlock the door to my heart
Best to speak wisely, stall a motor mouth's start
Confidence knows confidence,
And the offspring, together, each could bring

Making first expressions
Can be a telling thing
Making first impressions
Can make the bold or trepid heart sing

Aesthetic faculties
On sudden overdrive and overload
Absolutely astounded
By what my olfactory nerves and optics behold

Sober, awake yet dreaming
Better open the door to my heart
Slow motion is dream weaving
This tapestry's end may be its start

If it's all about procreation,
Casual sex reveals a human flaw
Preserving pearls for a better world
Requires prerequisites before the thaw

MANTLE

By Donald T. Williams

Gone are the years
And the fixture pictures on the mantle
Memories, awash in tears,
Drown emotions I can't handle

My musical friends
All lined in a row
Smile at me
Before each private show

Every time
So loud and true
They do for me
What real people can't or won't do

Photographs,
Audio stereo sound
Take spirits up
Take spirits down

CD's in the laser light
Shine
Giving life to souls
Trapped in plastic for time

Times like these
When I'm all alone
For times I should call
Because I sense you're home

Null and void
The comfy uncomfortable space
Cold
Without a comforting embrace

Photographs
Do fill the place
Singers, musicians, icons
Of all types and race

Multicultural collage
Created from the photos of a CD case
Make a fine, artistic facsimile,
But can't replace what I've somehow misplaced

Although safely secured,
Your image locked in a box
I never look upon it;
It's better that I not

Although I have your number
Die casted on my heart and brain
Each time I punch the digits
My fingers feel the pain

Like the needle prick
Of a blood testing kit
It hurts for an instance
And just a bit

I record the results
Time after time
Pick up my pen
Bleed another poem in rhyme

Testimony of my inevitable love
Peaks and valleys
Sweet and salty
As the sugar in my blood

Drop one addiction
For another disease
I am at peace
But never at ease

Times like these

When I'm all alone
For times I should call
Because I sense you're home

Null and void
The comfy, uncomfortable space
Cold
Without your comforting embrace

Gone are the years
And the fixture pictures on the mantle
Memories, awash in tears,
Drown emotions I can't handle

My musical friends
All lined in a row
Smile at me
Before each private show

Private Dancer
Knows her place
Tempest Snake
Is her base

Shadows dance
In a corner's light
Alone are we
Each and every night

Every time
So loud and true
They do for me
What real people can't or won't do

TIPPY TOE

By Donald T. Williams

My love is hers
I can't despise
I love her lips
Though wet with lies

In a corner
Is her place
Tempest Snake
Does make her base

Dance upon
Her tippy toe
Beneath her dress
Dost bottom show

In a swirl
Of figure eights
Upheld hoop
Dost tell of fate

Peer the fiery
Place so near
Circle in the square
Appears

There the square
In shadow makes state
Center
Of the triple eights

While tri sixes
You fixate
Turn the wheels
Of the triple eight

Turn like gears
On a Doom's Day clock
Like a shadow there
Then not

Ever see
An "S" reflect?
Looks the same
As one expects

Clever catch
The subtlety
SW/NE
Trickery

Subtle
As an abstruse smile
Like Mona Lisa's
Elusive guile

My love is hers
I can't despise
I love her lips
Though wet with lies

In a corner
Is her place
Tempest Snake
Does make her base

Dance upon
Her tippy toe
Beneath her dress
Dost bottom show

In a swirl
Of figure eights
Upheld hoop
Tells of our fate

Sidewinder's face
So close to sand
Leaves its mark
Without a hand

Where it goes
Shows where it's been
Disappears
By way of wind

Thus does swirl
The triple eights
Winds of change
No longer wait

While tri sixes
You fixate
Turn the wheels
Of the triple eight

Turn like gears
On a Doom's Day clock
Like a shadow there
Then not

I'VE A . . .

By Donald T. Williams

I've a hunger
I've a thirst
To get paid
For what I'm worth

Lay my life
And my health on the lie
To tell it straight
With truth in rhyme

Verbal barrage
Is what I cut loose
Loose lips sink ships
And some tie the noose

What I say
Is what I've said
What you read
Is what you've read

Take or leave
As grain of salt
Truth be told
Cannot be false

Death by cop
Or lack of bail
Same old tree
Just different nails

Through the hands
And through the feet
Through the heart
And, yet, it beats

Beats out truth
That never fails
And a voice
That both sings and wails

I've a hunger
I've a thirst
To get paid
For what I'm worth

Lay my life
And my health on the lie
To tell it straight
With truth in rhyme

What I say
May cook my goose
As is the case
When one speaks truth

History long
Has proven this
Many fine, dead men
Top the list

If it be
In millions, knives, noose, or gun
Only proves
I am "The One"

I've a hunger
I've a thirst
I've a mission purpose
Since my birth

Donald T. Williams

DROPPED MY ROCKS

By Donald T. Williams

Dropped my rocks
After twenty-five years
Didn't replace them with booze
Didn't replace them with beer

Didn't replace them with frivolous sex
Or immaterial material things
Looked up and hooked up
With the love God brings

Pipe had burned until red hot
Torched lips and hands but dropped it not
Loved the high and the lift
Didn't matter how much I hit

Grown man would not be told
How long or how far to go
It's my time, can pay for mine
So leave me alone

Until one day
How much was enough?
My life wasn't hard
My life wasn't rough

Dropped my rocks
After twenty-five years
Didn't replace them with booze
Didn't replace them with beer

Didn't replace them with frivolous sex
Or immaterial material things
Looked up and hooked up
With the love God brings

450

Pipe had burned
Until red hot
Wrecked my family
So I finally dropped

Until one day
Enough was enough
Wife's love turned cold
Sons stated disgust

Until one day
Enough was enough
My life became hard
My life became rough

What it was
Was one big lie
How I lived
Is how I'd die

Eyes once opened
I could see through the smoke
Anymore drags
Would make me croak

Dropped my rocks
After twenty-five years
Picked them up
Staring down the Devil's dare

Palm reader once told me
What my future was to be
What could and would happen
But I didn't heed

How life could be sunny
Or life could be blue
How things turn out
Depends on what you do

How could I take her
At her word?

451

Gypsies and palm readers
Are for the birds

Figured I was man enough
To call her bluff
Double-dare the Devil
Because it's God I trust

Time will tell
And prove to me
Just "who" knows
What is to be

Omnipotent God
Over ominous angel
Runs the whole show
Be no question which way to go

Gypsy once read
What was in my hand
What was in store
For an inquisitive man

What gypsy said
That she could see
Became for me
Reality

Many roads were taken
Ground beneath me was shaken
Folks around me were faking
And rude was wakening

Restored sensibility
Brought me humbly to my knees
Life half gone and on the brink
Still had brains with which to think

Best thing that ever happened for me
Was Jesus dying on that wicked tree
Just like Jesus bled and bled

I was brought back from the dead

Dead on the inside
All throughout
Body mostly water
With a desert's drought

Living Water came along
And offered a drink
Told me that my lungs were black,
But He could turn them pink

Fess up to my list of sins
And sin no more
Turn my back on rocks of crack
Have the Solid Rock as my floor

You can test the Devil
But with the Triple Threat
Please don't play

God has got this earth game won
Stand with Him and with the Son
Each and every day it pays
Can't begin to count the ways

Dropped my rocks
After twenty-five years
Didn't replace them with booze
Didn't replace them with beer

Didn't replace them with frivolous sex
Or immaterial material things
Looked up and hooked up
With the love God brings

What I write
Is how I sing
About Lord my God,
The King of Kings

GREY SPECTRE'S VERSE

By Donald T. Williams

When the Lord
Gives me a poem,
It's the marrow
Of the bone

It's the essence
Of DNA
It's the proton
Of subatomic play

Play on words
In rhyme and verse
Brevity
Concise and terse

Artfully,
I have my say
Have it not
No other way

Double negatives
Flippant tease
Mock of tongue
That slips with ease

Riddled enigma
Unrehearsed
True meanings
Are something worse

Decode, decipher
Cypher naught
Zero is the sum
You've got

Emptiness
The vacuum filled
Yet, my poems
You ponder still

When the Lord
Gives me a poem,
It's the marrow
Of the bone

It's the essence
Of DNA
It's the proton
Of subatomic play

Why leave thoughts
In disarray?
Confusion masked
As night and day?

Sense of order
Disguised as time
Only order
Lies in my rhymes

Rhymes and rhythm
Given me by my Lord
Musical composition
In each verse and chord

Artfully,
I have my say
Have it not
No other way

Double negatives
Flippant tease
Mock of tongue
That slips with ease

455

Words of Wisdom
May dismay
That's the way
Grey Spectre plays

Those who read
Each verse and line
Get the drift
Between the rhyme

Come away
With something learned
Lamps are lit
As knowledge burns

When the Lord
Gives me a poem,
It's the marrow
Of the bone

Bloodshed gift
Dripped from His throne
Take my word
Truth as I know

Grey Spectre
Speaks with tongue in cheek
May sound funny
May sound bleak

Never promised
Balms to soothe
Only promised
Pearls of truth

Take and read
Or leave as found
From the Lord
These poems drip down

It's the essence
Of DNA
It's the proton
Of subatomic play

Play on words
In rhyme and verse
Brevity
Concise and terse

Artfully,
I have my say
Have it not
No other way

Riddled enigma
Unrehearsed
True meanings
Or something worse

Decode, decipher
Cypher naught
Zero is the sum
You've got

Emptiness
The vacuum filled
Yet, my poems
You ponder still

Words of Wisdom
May dismay
That's the way
Grey Spectre plays

Those who read
Each verse and line
Get the drift
Between the rhyme

Come away
With something learned
Lamps are lit
As knowledge burns

Artfully,
I have my say
Have it not
No other way

Emptiness
The vacuum filled
Yet, my poems
You ponder still

SUNNY-SIDE UP

By Donald T. Williams

Grey Spectre's with me
Surfing on the wind
Grey Spectre's drifting
Going forth to where he's been

Time may be a circle
As oval as the ellipse
Darkening ring of fire
As sun and moon eclipse

Life may be a yoke
Center of egg within
Sunny-side up of breakfast
As each new day begins

Yokes are made to be broken
Consumed as nourishing
Weight once off the shoulders
Release life's burdens strengthening

Dimming lights once cut off
May brighten once again
Center has no middle
Middle has no end

Grey Spectre's with me
Surfing on the wind
Grey Spectre's drifting
Going forth to where he's been

Time may be a circle
As oval as the ellipse
Darkening ring of fire
As sun and moon eclipse

How removed from eclogue
Are the verses of these poems!
Yet, the shepherds dialogue
In controversial verses as of song

Far removed from eclogue
Are the verses of these poems!
Yet, ellipses aren't in remiss
Blank spaces are not wrong

Sure as God's in Heaven yet everywhere at home
Grey Spectre has made himself known
Sure as Jesus is in Heaven yet everywhere at dome
Grey Spectre's with me, I'm never alone

Most unlikely herders or fishermen of men
The "city boy" in a rustic realm
God has set my course for me
Jesus is at the helm

Life may be a yoke
Center of an egg within
Sunny-side up of breakfast
As each new day begins

Yokes are made to be broken
Consumed as nourishing
Weight once off the shoulders
Releases life's strengthening

Eclosion is a cycle
Mother Nature at her best
Works well for the adult insect
Emerging from the pupal case or egg of rest

I was once a child
Now I am a man
Lessons learned the hard way
Best remembered by those who can

My hope to forgive
My dope to forget
Better days lie before me
Sunny-side up, all the better yet

Grey Spectre's with me
Surfing on the wind
Grey Spectre's drifting
Going forth to where he's been

Most unlikely herders or fishermen of men
The "city boy" in a rustic realm
God has set my course for me
Jesus is at the helm

GOD IS LOVE

By Donald T. Williams

Now that I have written
What I have to say
Donnie C is willing
To forgive and walk to or away

Willing to bury his pistol, knife, and tongue
That can slice and dice
Willing to forgive and forget
To move forward in his life

Are you also willing
To let me off the hook?
Are you also willing
To close the cover on this book?

If this is the closure
That you are seeking too,
Perhaps there is now a "pow wow"
That we can sit down to?

I would be so grateful
If God would mend our hearts
I would be so thankful
If we didn't live apart

Miracles can and do happen
For wretches such as us
God has all the answers
And it's His will I trust

In truth, I still love you
Have and always will
I know you still love me
It moves me when I'm still

God is love
Love is God
God means business,
Won't spare the rod

Love leaves you holy
In more ways than one
Tough love is serious
Tough love isn't fun

Donnie C's learned a hard lesson
Donnie C knows the immense cost
There's hope for the separated
Hope to find a love once lost

ABOUT THE AUTHOR

When I reflect on my baby boomer childhood and youth, I consider myself fortunate in that I was raised by loving, hardworking parents who strived to better themselves and give their four children a satisfactory life. I recall finally growing tall enough to see out of our ninth floor apartment windows and the fanciful time spent daydreaming about what it will take to someday buy a home like the ones across the street and to park my cars outside. The Albany Projects of Brooklyn, NY was a tough place to grow up during the late fifties on into the sixties but love lived there and that made it home. Family, good neighbors, and good friends made my immediate world a basically pleasant place despite the possible dangers lying within and beyond the domain and surrounding territory of the Albany Chaplins. According to the gang members I revered but was never completely accepted by, I was College Boy, Mrs. Williams' son. I was the kid who could hang on the fringes of thug life until his curfew time. Holding my Orange Rock, hitting and passing the joint, but most importantly, "passing on those chucks like a motherfucker", I had a place at the concrete checker and chess tables of St. Johns Park next to the OG's who looked out for me because I made them money and a bit for myself. I was Mr. Williams' son at a time when "very bad" young men weren't so bad and still respected their elders and a man's family. Being half ass in things like basketball, ranking, street fighting, and school work had its merits, but my father in his circle was good with cards and I in my circle was good with dice. Somehow, I think that saved me a few butt whippings in the park but very few at home. I often stole money from my father and mother to make more money gambling and it broke their hearts until one day I acknowledged their tears of pain and I stopped. Stopped stealing from them at least but never stopped gambling or any of the street hustling ventures of the day.

What I did manage to do was graduate from high school, land a praiseworthy job, with the US Postal Service and serve as a window clerk in my neighborhood Post Office. It was my first full-time job after graduating and my mother was proud. She was even prouder when I entered The City College of New York, met my college sweetheart whom I married, graduated from CCNY, and was hired by the NYC Board of Education as a teacher for thirty three years. Attending the New School for Social Research in New York City and graduating from Wesleyan University in Middleton, Connecticut with a Master's Degree was an experience I'll always cherish. Somehow, living a double life worked for me. Being a College Boy, street hustler, and married man paid dividends and my wife, who also earned a career in education and conquered the challenges of administration, liked the stability and all the little extras I would dole on her because that's what a man does. He takes care of his lady and his mistresses too. As in any relationship, there were rough patches, mostly made rocky by me, but I married young against my wise mother's and Smokey's advice. I did a lot of "shopping around" after the fact and can only blame myself for messing up a good thing. A woman scorned is one of nature's sneakiest creatures I've sadly discovered. Lessons learned from the snake I imagine. Mine might have waited decades or could have been getting even all along. Truth is I took my eyes off the prize. In any case, when she decided to break free after thirty three years, I suppose I got what I deserved but if you asked me, I'd have to say it was overkill. Like the singer, Blu Cantrell sang, "If he mess up, you got to hit 'em up" and I was shot down, left for dead, and forgotten before I hit the dirt. My daddy used to say, "The bitch ain't been born who can take my money" and my aunt used to say, "A woman can wrap and sell a nigger in a minute". I respected their frankness and wisdom. So as far as I'm concerned, I "chivalrously" let her have my dough and didn't mind the plain brown paper she wrapped and sent me packing in because after all, I did and do love her. She will always be my wife, and I will always be her husband, good, bad, and grotesque. Once, when I was locked up a few years ago, a couple of young brothers having a discussion asked, "Pops, can you turn a "ho" into a housewife?" and my reply was, "No, but who can be sure about any person?" Having been married, separated and divorced from one or none of the aforementioned, I spoke truthfully from experience and firsthand knowledge. Continue reading, living, learning, and tripping on the bittersweet tab or cube of life. You'll understand my reasoning. Watch your step.

TO ORDER ADDITIONAL COPIES OF:

THE DEVIL MADE ME DO IT TOO

Please forward your check or money order (plus shipping and handling) to:

GREY SPECTRE ENTERPRISE, LLC
DONALD T. WILLIAMS
P.O. BOX 71955 Henrico, VA 23225
(web address) www.greyspectrenterprises.com